Estate Agent's Secrets

The Hidden Secrets
The Top Performers In The Industry
Don't Want You To Know
(they work for letting agents too...)

Volume II - Engage

Silas J. Lees

ESTATE AGENT'S SECRETS

The Hidden Secrets The Top Performers In The Industry
Don't Want You To Know
(they work for letting agents too...)

Volume II - Engage

ISBN: 9798841260509

This publication is designed to provide accurate and authoritative information regarding the subject matter covered. It is sold with the understanding that the publisher is not engaged in rendering legal, accounting, or other professional services. If you require legal advice or other expert assistance, you should seek the services of a competent professional.

Disclaimer: The author makes no guarantees to the results you'll achieve by reading this book. All business requires risk and hard work. Your results may vary when undertaking any new business venture or marketing strategy.

DEDICATION

We dedicate the estate agent's secrets book series to all those people who are determined enough to make their dreams come true. Those of you who continually face uphill struggles, setbacks, and disappointments in life, yet keep on going no matter what.

The road to personal and business success is long and winding; full of learning opportunities which bring challenges and frustrations, yet those determined souls who keep digging deep and keep trying 'just one more time' know, that one day soon, it will all be worthwhile.

You are the true heroes in life and our source of inspiration. Thank you for being all that you are.

Welcome to the Property Revolution, we're just getting started.

DISCLAIMER

Unfortunately, in today's litigious society, we must state that the ideas shared within this book do not, in any way, constitute financial advice and we are not regulated by the FCA or any other financial or other professional regulated authority.

We're not qualified to make any such claims regarding the merits or otherwise of a particular investment, particularly within an economy that is greatly uncertain at the time of writing (March 2022).

We encourage all parties reading our books to seek sound and competent financial guidance from a suitably qualified professional in accordance with the law. We also encourage all parties to seek sound and competent legal guidance from suitably qualified lawyers.

The author and WiggyWam Limited, it's directors or employees cannot, and will not, be held responsible for any errors or omissions contained within this book and share the information contained within as ideas and suggestions only.

Finally, it's fair to say we're not professional writers, and there will be some small errors and omissions within the text. We ask that you take the substance of the book on board rather than getting caught up in the small detail that detracts from your learning.

CONTENTS

INTRODUCTION

MORE SECRETS YOU'VE BEEN WAITING FOR...

By now, you should have read the first Volume in the estate agents secret's trilogy and you're well on your way to implementing all the great secret strategies you've learnt so far.

If you're diving into this volume without at least making a start on the hard yards involved in getting the foundation right in your business, we must insist you go back and complete this vital work as we'll be building on it throughout this volume. It will also become crucial when we get stuck into Volume III as we don't want your business to fall over once you've flooded it with work.

Fair warning, ok?

This second part of your learning journey will help you understand how to build that deep connection with prospects, so they choose you to the exclusion of all others. Sabri Suby explains it best when he says most business owners get their marketing wrong because they're focused all their efforts on the 3% of buyers who are ready to buy right now.

But the other 97% of buyers are largely ignored!

So, this Volume will focus on how to nurture that 97% in a low-cost way, so that you're the automatic choice when they're ready to pull the trigger on a buying decision. If you focus your efforts on this untapped 97%, how much bigger do you think your organisation can grow, when you've got to where you are by competing for the 3% of ready buyers in the bloodbath which is fighting tooth and nail against your competition?

And by the end of this book, you'll see why we've structured these volumes the way we have – quick and easy reads with plenty of juicy secrets to implement into your business today.

If you haven't got all three Volumes – here's the link to grab them now so you won't miss out on any vital secret that could make all the difference to your business:

http://www.wiggywam.co.uk/estateagentssecretstrilogy

We strongly suggest you guard these books with your life!

As with Volume I, as you go through this book, the work will present you with many questions, so it's important to write them down for two reasons:

1) A question running round in your head will distract you, so you may overlook some priceless gems because you're not fully focused on the secrets we're sharing with you.

2) You might get overwhelmed by thinking "How do I do this…?" and then putting the book to one side because it seems a little complicated, or worse, you run off to Google the 'How To…' and get sucked into all sorts of different avenues which waste lots of time but won't actually move the needle in your business.

We promise you that all the answers to your questions can be found within the pages of this book and the other two volumes, and we want you to hold us to that promise! So, our best advice it to write your questions down as they come up and then tick them off as you get the answers later on.

And if you need any extra help in implementing these secrets, we're only a short email away – HappyToHelp@WiggyWam.co.uk

Or you can book in a free 30-minute consultation if you want to know how you can really add value to your clients and your business. There's a ton of extra resources we can share with you on a call.

Here's the link to book:

http://www.wiggywam.co.uk/estateagentssecretscall

Getting Stuck In

As a reminder, here's the promises we made to you at the start of Volume I:

1) To deliver value far in excess of the purchase price (a minimum 10x return on your investment – think buying £1,000 note for only £100).

2) The opportunity to increase your fees to a level not seen before within your practice (and above that of your competition).

3) As well as raising your fees, we'll also show you how to win more instructions.

4) Reduce timescales for your property deals, so you get paid far more quickly and reduce the burden on your cashflow.

5) As a result of increased fees and reduced timescales for your deals, the natural consequence is increased profits in your business at the end of the trading year. As you'll discover later, this can automatically increase the value of your company by a factor of three!

6) With increased profits, you'll be able to afford better quality staff and better systems, so you'll enjoy working less hours on the coalface of the business and have more time to focus on the important work, (leaving you less stressed).

7) As a result of all of the above, your business should be well run, leaving you with peace of mind and enjoying more of the trappings of success.

These are significant promises to make and we certainly wouldn't be making them if we didn't feel that we could back them up by sharing all of our expert knowledge and hidden secrets.

More importantly, we're providing the secret roadmap to help quickly improve the profitability of your business. So do yourself a favour: make a commitment to finish this book and the others in the series if you want the results you're searching for.

(Another bonus secret for agents is to get an "Accountability Partner" in your pursuit of this roadmap. If you have a trusted agency friend who you also think would benefit from the same goals, we encourage you to get them on board with your learning journey, so you have someone to bounce ideas off and get into the detail with.

So, send them to http://www.wiggywam.co.uk/estateagentssecretstrilogy and make a commitment to one another that you'll hold each other accountable to your promises of both finishing AND IMPLEMENTING the secret roadmap to agency success.

We also have a fast-track 12-week accountability program to help you implement all these secrets into your business, so reach out to us if you think we can help – HappyToHelp@WiggyWam.co.uk)

A Quick Reminder

No doubt you've tried to solve the problems in your business on your own, or you've read some books by industry experts, or you've even gone on some webinars or seminars to learn from those people who tell you they know more than you.

But there's one thing which no-one has shared with you, and that's the secret treasure map to help you find your way to the riches you desire.

Bad analogy? Not at all.

You see, we're willing to bet that trying to solve the biggest challenge in your business, is as frustrating as it is futile, and the reason for that is, it's not just one problem you need to solve, much to the dismay of all the "experts" out there telling you to solve one issue and all your dreams will come true. The harsh truth is, there's no point in trying to generate more leads for your business if your conversion rate to new instructions is pitifully low. There's no point trying to 'learn social media' when your business doesn't effectively deal with the gold mine of opportunity its currently sitting on.

What you need, which these series of books are all about, is presenting this secret roadmap which takes you through a nine-step process to get you from Point A to Point B, and which leaves no stone unturned in your pursuit of excellence. And if you're already feeling overwhelmed at what could be a huge task, don't worry as we've got you covered. We've done as much of the work as possible to give you all the tools, knowledge, and information necessary to transform your business from run-of-the-mill, to the best agency in town.

The only thing required from you at this stage is to just commit to the process and trust that what we're taking you through will be to your ultimate benefit. Suspend your ego and turn down the volume on the negative voice in your head that says, "I already know this" because – as the old saying goes - 'To know, and not to do, is not yet to know.'

We trust you'll set aside the idea of indulging in mental masturbation to intellectually understand this information, and instead, get your hands dirty as you embrace a new way of doing things that will make a huge difference to your business.

Now if all this seems a little too much, take inspiration from the face that you competition will still be doing what everyone else is doing and most likely won't bother picking up this book or exploring the information further through our other training, resources, or learning centre. Besides which, literally nobody else in the industry is teaching this depth of information, so you're already ahead of like 95% of other agents out there.

And for that, we salute you! But don't rest on your laurels – Take ACTION!

It is our deep desire to make sure you get phenomenal value out of this book; much more than the cost of buying it. To that end, we've done our best to go above and beyond the call of duty in delivering the cutting edge thinking from not just within the agency industry, but further afield. We think you'll be amazed by some of the strategies we share with you, but not only that, we're going to help you implement what you learn.

As the saying goes, 'ideas are a dime a dozen, its effective execution that makes them valuable'. We couldn't agree more, so let's get cracking on this exciting journey together.

Finally, we were going to make this offer at the back of each book as a reward for those readers who took the time to seek out all the key learnings and implement them in their business. However, realising how busy we all are, and the uphill struggle we're all going to be faced with as we head out of the pandemic, (into potentially World War Three and as out-of-control inflation begins to bite), we wanted to try and help as many people as possible put these learnings into practice in their business.

So, as a reward for simply buying this book, and for being the forward-thinking agent you are, we'd like to offer you exclusive access to a highly effective training course which will literally take you by the hand and walk you through each of the ideas presented here to help you rapidly implement them within your business.

The key focus of the training is to:

1. Help you win more instructions
2. Help you increase your fees
3. To flood your pipeline with more (profitable), work than you can handle
4. Reduce your stress and workload

This exclusive closed-door training is valued at over £5,000 and we have limited seats available to service the high level of demand we're experiencing as a result of publishing this book.

To be honest with you, this is not your average training and requires us to dedicate a huge amount of personal time and resources to support agents in their journey to become the best agent in their area, so don't know how long we'll be able to make this available for, or how many people we can realistically accommodate (it won't be many).

So, if you'd like to grab one of the last remaining seats, simply email us: HappyToHelp@WiggyWam.co.uk with the heading; "Make me a VIP" for the opportunity to get on board whilst it's still available.

Helping Others

Once you've received value from this book, we'd really appreciate you recommending it to a fellow agent, friend, or relative in the industry who can also take the opportunity to grow and expand their business. We trust they'll find much greater value in the secrets shared than the cost of this book.

BUT, if you truly want to help them, **don't** give them this book for free…

Here's why…

For some bizarre reason, humans will take action to hoard a precious resource, but won't necessarily take action to use that resource, especially if they had to exert little effort to obtain it. Think about how many times you've grabbed free stuff off the internet and never read it because it wasn't a high enough priority to read it during your busy day.

So, if you give this away for free, the odds are against your friend ever using it. We didn't design human psychology, it's just the way it is – if you truly want to help them, get them to buy the book by sending them to: http://www.wiggywam.co.uk/estateagentssecretstrilogy

Also, if you like the idea of being rewarded and learning more, please find the time to leave an honest review on Amazon, to not only inspire other people, but to give us the opportunity to bring more learnings, knowledge, and wisdom to you in future editions. Your clients, your industry, and you yourself deserve the best, so thank you for striving to be the best of the best.

Finally, if you have any suggestions on how we can improve these books, or to share lessons learnt or helpful stories to assist others, please get in touch via: HappyToHelp@WiggyWam.co.uk

We look forward to working with you very soon,

Silas and all the team at WiggyWam.

Welcome to the Property Revolution, we're just getting started

CHAPTER ONE

SALES SECRETS

How Are You doing?

As you start the journey into the second volume of these books, we thought we'd check in with you to see how you're doing? There can be a lot of information and new ideas to take in so don't worry if you're feeling a little overwhelmed as this is where the rubber meets the road.

Volume I took you on quite a journey to understand the type of problems that exist within the industry and then looked at how to create a more solid foundation in your business to launch the new breed of agency. Throughout this volume, all will become clear why we've chosen to structure the three books in this way.

We highly recommend making a ton of notes as you work through Volume II, because if you've been paying attention, your brain should be firing with all sorts of different ideas about how you can beat the competition hands down. And that should give you the motivation to keep working through this book, but more importantly, implementing what we're sharing with you. There's surely no finer motivation than the inspiration which hits you from a good idea you know your clients will love and embracing the tireless work ethic that springs forth to just get the job done!

We felt the best way to structure this book was to focus on the improvements you can make in the processes you've currently got working for you when it comes to customer acquisition. We'll look at how most agents typically operate, and what we can do to stack the odds in your favour to win business time and again in the face of stiff competition.

We'll also review best practice in the profession and how agents at the top of their game are gaining the unfair advantage in client acquisition, client retention and referrals.

So, without further ado, strap on your seatbelts and let's dive in...

The Smart Agent's SECRET Black Book

In this section, we're going to look at what we consider to be your new sales engine within your business, or Sales 2.0 as we call it. We've detailed as much information as possible to show you how to crush any objection, win more business, and close more deals in record time. We'll also share with you proven secrets, hints, tips, techniques, and rebuttals to help you along.

What we're sharing here is based on 25+ years' experience in the property industry where we've used this specific information to sell millions of pounds worth of homes to buyers, win millions of pounds worth of new instructions, get people to sell their properties to us, get tenants to take a rental on their first viewing and even to sell millions of pounds worth of property investment education and training.

For most of you reading this, you'll be familiar with a certain way of doing things to try and win new business and close deals. What we've seen far too often however, is agents willing to slash fees to win instructions, rather than having the faith and confidence in themselves to differentiate their service enough to charge what they're really worth.

When we first started in estate agency in the late 1990's, we were always told:

"If you can't negotiate a good fee for your services, what chance have you got of negotiating the best possible deal for your clients?"

These words echoed in our ears every time there was a temptation to cut fees to win business. It's hard; especially when you're faced with an environment where your competition does cut fees or overvalues properties purposely. Or more often than not, does both.

And yet, the solution can be so easy that many mistakenly overlook its power and instead retreat to what they already know; competing by; overvaluing the property and cutting fees as we touched on in Volume I. The secret comes down to literally one thing: **perceived value**.

Notice the words.

Perceived.

Value.

Value is always subjective, but ultimately if you can create the perception of **significant value** in any transaction, your clients will willingly pay the price you ask.

If you're sick and tired of being on the merry-go-round to nowhere and want to finally start earning your worth whilst dominating your competition, then read on.

WARNING!

The secret strategies, tips, and techniques you'll encounter are VERY powerful and must not be used dishonestly or to cheat people in any way. The mantra you should have in mind at all times is this:

"How Can I Help These People?"

This will keep you on the straight and narrow path and guide your actions towards genuinely helping your clients to achieve their goals and dreams, (with your expert assistance of course), EVEN IF it means you recommend your potential client places their business elsewhere, or you don't offer to sell your services to them when its ethically or morally right to do so.

Keeping this mantra in mind ourselves, we wanted to offer our readers as much value as possible, so forgive us that the original book has ballooned from the originally planned one hundred pages, to the three volumes it is today. We're certain you'll find plenty of value.

A Word Or Two About Value

One of the biggest frustrations ever shared by agents is the mistaken belief that the general public won't pay higher fees, and as your competitors are all charging less, the default position is to reduce your own fees to be competitive enough to win instructions. We're going to be bold enough to tell you that this objection, like the prison of the Matrix, exists only in your mind.

The problem is simply that you are not showing your potential clients enough perceived value to justify a higher fee. Focus on the words 'perceived value' in that sentence as you read it again.

What Is Perceived Value?

The perception of value is subjective, depending upon the individual. Think about what is arguably one of the greatest symbols of wealth in the world, a Rolls-Royce. Now to some people, such a car represents significant value. The quality of the materials. The design and engineering that's gone into it. The exclusivity of driving a world-renown marque that few can afford.

And for those people, the price tag is a bargain.

But if you look at a Rolls-Royce and compare it to, say a Ford Focus, and you're comparing the fact that they both have four wheels, both get you from A to B and both keep the wind and rain out, you're going to have a very hard time justifying the extra spend on buying a Roller.

They're both a car, but there's two totally different perceptions of value.

So, what does this have to do with estate agency?

Well- think about the service you're offering and how it stacks up against your competition. How does your service compare to the perceived market leaders such as Savills and Knight Frank? Are you offering more perceived value than they are, or are you undercutting them on fees because you don't feel you can compete head-to-head?

In our experience, a professional, local estate agent can outperform the 'big boys' if they know what they're doing. When we sold a farmhouse and barn conversion complex a few years ago, Savills' representative made us feel like they weren't interested in selling the properties; undervaluing them and throwing a cheap fee at the job when we told them their valuation was (a lot), less than we were expecting.

A professional local agent sold the properties for £100,000 more than the Savills' valuation, and we willingly paid them a higher fee for doing so. Perversely, the local agent was therefore the "cheapest" because they helped realise so much extra value.

Perceived Value. So, we had no arguments about paying the higher fee.

So, the question is, where are you underselling yourself?

A Dose Of Reality

The general public do not mind paying for things which offer value. That said, you won't find 100% of people are the right fit for your business, so you should only focus on the target market where you can offer great value to a group of prospects who are willing and able to pay a higher fee for your services.

Let's step back for a second and think about the important role an estate agent has in the life of a potential client. You literally have the power to influence where people live, what price they achieve in the sale of their property, and how that will impact on the purchase of their next home. Your role even helps to shape their future and may help a client get close to the right school for their children or be closer to work so they can cut down on stressful commuting, so their home life is better, or a dozen other things which we often take for granted.

When it comes to the selling price of your clients' home, offering value is of paramount importance. Being at the top of your game, you make the difference between a move being profitable for your client, or one that could be very expensive. Offers that you achieve more than the asking price through skilful marketing and a competitive viewing and offer process, can greatly impact the personal finances of your clients. Don't forget, you're dealing with tens, if not hundreds of thousands of pounds, and some of you in the millions.

We can hear you saying, "Yes Silas, I already know this! Tell me something I don't know!"

Well consider this; most of your competition are all operating in the same way. Booking the market appraisal, attending the property, looking around, providing a valuation, pitching their fee and then hoping they win the business. And out of every 3 agents that attend the property, you've got about a 33% chance of being selected as the winning agent, all things being equal.

Let's take this a step further. Detach yourself from your current position and put yourself in your client's shoes for a moment to think about what grounds a potential client has to distinguish between one agent and another. It's harder than you think to do this exercise. It will pay you to draw up a comparison chart between you and your competitors and look at each individual distinguishing point to see how you really differ from your competition. Is it the quality of your advertising? Is it your funky new website? Is it the fact that you offer accompanied viewings if a client cannot be there to show people around (or doesn't want to)? Or is it the fact that you have the most boards up in your local area?

If you're honest with yourself and can really step back from your position, you'll see that in reality, your potential prospect, doesn't understand the true difference between one agent and another.

Prospects can only form an opinion on a very short customer journey; booking the valuation appointment, experiencing the agent inspecting their home, and the follow up marketing report they receive. That's pretty much it. Sure, they might check out your website and your press advertising, maybe even your shop window, but you're leaving a lot to chance as far as winning their business is concerned.

So how does this lead us to being able to distinguish ourselves from our competition and win higher fees? It comes down to the perception your client has of you against the background of your competition. And where, in the eyes of your client, you are all perceived to be the same, the client has very little option other than to go with whoever says they will get the most for their home, and who will charge the least for doing so.

Never forget, that your client is unlikely to make the connection with the "cheapest agent" **being the one that costs the least**, because they help achieve the highest sale price and therefore pay for themselves many times over. It is very difficult for a client to discern between agents, especially when some may be guilty of overvaluing. This is why your competition 'gets away' with this tired tactic time and time again, because the client has such limited information over a short period of time upon which to base their decision.

If you want to know how you can really add value to your clients and your business, there's a ton of extra resources we can share with you on a call.

We just ask you to invest 30 minutes into a complimentary consultation, where we can help fast-track your success (with no hard sell whatsoever).

Here's the link to book your call:

http://www.wiggywam.co.uk/estateagentssecretscall

CHAPTER TWO

THE MOST OVERLOOKED SECRET IN AGENCY

A bold statement, we realise, however let's look at why selling your services to your potential clients seems to be so hard. And it's this:

What you're selling isn't tangible.

Your potential client can't really touch it, taste it, smell it, or even see it.

It's not like selling a Rolls-Royce where you can get the client to sit in the car and to feel the supple leather of the seats supporting them perfectly in their driving position as they whizz along the road at sixty miles an hour with the only sound they can hear being the ticking of the beautifully designed analogue clock occupying pride of place on the dashboard…

That's tangible. That's something people can equate to value. So how do you sell an intangible like a service? Well, it's your job to **educate your potential client**, over and over if necessary, to ensure they make the right decision when it comes to selecting the best agent (you) to help them sell their home.

Yet to be successful, you must do things very differently to your competition. And generally speaking, you must start your client's education journey much earlier on in the process; well <u>before</u> they are even <u>thinking</u> about selling their home. When you do this effectively, you'll be the <u>only</u> obvious choice in your marketplace. But to do so, will require you to operate in a way that's almost counter opposite to your competition, and that can be a lonely journey.

Are you willing to take some risks so you can benefit from the rewards? Even better, it will take a long time for your competition to catch on, and when they do, you'll have already established a healthy head-start. At best, they can then only ever be perceived as a poor imitation of you.

The First Step On A Lonely Journey

Taking the first step on this journey is going to require putting in some hard yards outside of your normal day-to-day activities, if you want to build up a superior customer service experience your clients enjoy which ultimately positions you as the go-to expert in your local market.

One of the most overlooked points by agents is the fact that most people move house, on average, every 23 years! When you're in the day-to-day business of selling homes, your knowledge in this area and how to navigate the stresses and strains of doing so, is incredibly valuable. However, such specialist knowledge, is not in your client's possession and without it, they're prey to all sorts of pitfalls, difficulties, and manipulations, (such as choosing your competition for example!).

When you demonstrate your extensive knowledge to your potential clients (which to you may seem very simple), it will be perceived as a revelation and incredibly useful to help them navigate the third most stressful thing they can go through in their lives. Think about the following and how you can position yourself in front of your client to answer these questions:

1) What should anyone consider when going through the process of choosing an estate agent? (This will be harder than you think to answer outside of repeating "the agent with the most boards" or "choose one that's on Rightmove" etc. Be original.)
2) Why cheap agent fees might be more expensive than you think.
3) Why overvaluing their home can cause a client to miss out on the home of their dreams.
4) The importance of providing buyers with up-front information to prevent a possible sale from falling through later on.
5) How to choose the right solicitor to handle the sale, and why choosing the cheapest will leave you unhappy, frustrated, needing therapy, and potentially losing the home of your dreams. (This might mean not using the solicitor you get paid the highest referral fee from).

9

6) The hazards and pitfalls of negotiating and how your clients can bring in a heavyweight expert in this field to fight their corner for them (you).

7) The most important things to bear in mind when selling your home to help you achieve the best possible price.

Emotions -vs- Logic

As an expert in human behaviour, you'll know that people can all be very different. They make different decisions based on the same information whilst some use logic in decision-making whilst others use their emotions to make their decisions for them.

What most don't realise however, is that almost **all people** make emotional decisions first, and then justify that decision using logic. So, you need to help your clients by giving them the right information to logically justify the emotional decision to choose you as their preferred agent.

Why Are You Telling Me This?

The secret shortcut to overcoming client objections is for those objections to not raise their ugly head in the first place! Otherwise, your pitch for their business turns into a live 'Whack-A-Mole' game with the client playing cat and mouse with their potential instruction.

So, the only way to prevent those objections being raised, which stops a client from automatically working with you (because they're all secretly terrified of getting screwed), is to provide a customer education and nurturing process that will prove your value to your client ahead of time so you become desirable to work with and the client willingly gives their business to you, rather than having to coax clients by overvaluing their home and cutting your fees.

Whilst your competition focusses on trying to win the business during and after the valuation, with the power of technology and a little bit of creative writing and video time, you'll be laying the foundations to win the business before your client even thinks about moving home.

Look at the needs of your inexperienced client, then provide the content and educational materials necessary to help them, so when they come to sell, you'll be at the front of their mind as they will already have had more tangible insights into your service and expert knowledge than that of your competition.

Only 8% Of Sellers Are Cost-Conscious

In a recent survey WiggyWam conducted with the home buying and selling public, we were shocked to discover only 8% of people were cost-conscious when it comes to moving home. This is contrary to what we always 'knew'; people were cost-sensitive and wanted to scrimp and save as many pennies along the way as possible because moving home is not cheap.

Wrong!

What's most revealing was the fact that people are prepared to pay **more** for services which make their moving experience smoother and hassle-free. And most importantly of all, **which educates them about what's involved in all the different processes**.

How could you use that knowledge and information in your business? And how could you increase your service offering and fees accordingly? Take some time to reflect on these questions now and write some ideas down. They could be instrumental in creating a massive USP between you and your competition.

Be warned however, we're not talking about the generic, lame content that clogs up the internet like, 'The latest trends in wallpaper designs'. Offer real, hard-hitting advice that can really help your potential clients. They're about to embark on one of the most expensive journeys of their lives and could be out of pocket if they get it wrong. So, help them.

You Never Get A Second-Chance To Make A Good First Impression

First impressions count for a lot in today's world. Unfortunately, we're all walking around with a silent judge, jury & executioner chattering away in our ears as we go about our daily lives. Can you hear it? It's probably the voice that's saying, 'I don't have that voice!' or words to that effect…

When it comes to winning over clients, we have to respect the fact that they're going to judge us within the first ten seconds of meeting us, and if we're trying to secure their business, we need to make those first ten seconds' count.

Coming back to our Rolls-Royce analogy, there's a reason why such cars are sold in expensive showrooms with well-polished sales professionals dressed in expensive suits who have mastered the art of persuasive sales. Have you noticed they're not sold out of dirty, back-road garage forecourts with 'Del-Boy' type salespeople wearing sheepskin coats, smoking cigars, and saying pretty much anything in order to secure a sale? Why do you think that is?

Again, perceived value.

So, when it comes to you, your services, and your offices, what first impression are you making? Do your staff look professional, smartly dressed in suitable business attire, and appropriately branded for the respective image you wish to convey? Or is the office in disarray with your staff dressed in cheap, ill-fitting garments which project the image that your company perhaps couldn't care less?

Or is it kind-of ok, but could do better?

We're always amazed when walking into an agent's office (and trust us, we've been in hundreds across the country), that so many of them look tired, dated, and lacklustre, when a fresh coat of paint, new carpets and a bit of staff training could really bring the office, and the agent's business, back to life.

It's even more surprising when you consider that most agents have referred tons of work to local tradespeople and could easily call in a few favours to help get their office looking incredible for not a lot of money…

Take a step back from your business, your office and your staff and ask yourself, is this really the image you want to convey to your clients? And if it's not, write down what you'd like to change to breathe new life into the professional image you'd ideally like to create. After all, the highest likelihood of making the most amount of money in agency comes from charging higher fees (or getting massive kickbacks from referral fees, something that's morally questionable in our view), and to charge higher fees, your business needs to look the part.

Location, Location, Location

Recently, there's been a trend of agents moving away from the High Street and into offices out of the town centre. The main reason seems to be to save costs, particularly when agents believe that placing properties on the internet does the same job as their shop window…

But there's more to an office than just a shop window. It's a place where clients can come to discuss their property problems and concerns (if they feel invited to do so). A place where they can receive a helping hand and guidance in navigating the moving minefield. And where they can see first-hand, their property is displayed in your shop window (a more common concern than most agents realise), and that you're being pro-active in promoting it for sale.

As a quick share, we once bought a £125,000 property for £86,000 from a couple who called us **after** instructing an agent to market their home. The agent had taken sales details, but after three weeks, there was no For Sale board, no window advertising, nor was it on the internet. The final straw was the client walking into the agent's office to ask the staff for details of their property, only to be told they didn't have a property for sale on that road…

If you're still intent on being away from the High Street, your corporate image can only be interpreted by the house buying and selling public through online or virtual mediums, so your telephone and email etiquette becomes far more important, as does your online presence. **IF** you want to charge the best fees that is. Otherwise, you're lost in the obscurity of being just another online agent "who puts all their properties on the internet," and there's plenty that will sell a property for near enough free nowadays, so how do you stand out against a backdrop of mediocrity?

In short, create that great first impression at every possible touchpoint a client may have with you and your company; from the way your staff are trained and the expertise they have, their telephone and email manner, your sales particulars, boards, viewing appointments, shop window, online presence, press advertising and the cars you drive.

Winning The Business

When it comes to making money in agency, the biggest opportunity most agents get is winning the instruction to list a new property **AND** getting it successfully sold, exchanged, and completed so they can invoice for their fee.

Unfortunately, a lot of agents mistakenly believe that just listing a property online and then agreeing a sale is most of their work done. They hand the memorandum of sale over to the solicitors and wait until they can send in the invoice for their fee. Not only is this wrong, but it's also a shoddy approach to estate agency and a poor attitude when they ought to be doing the best possible job they can for their client.

It seems like this has become more commonplace over the last ten years and a lot of agents overlook the most valuable part of their service: keeping the agreed sale together and getting it across the finishing line to the legal exchange of contracts. It's here where an agent's skills of negotiation are put to the test and dictates whether their client successfully moves home or has a ton of professional services bills to pay but is still stuck in the same home at the end of a dreadful and highly stressful experience.

So, the value a professional agent adds to a transaction can help them win future business, purely through the service they deliver to a buyer who is buying a property through them. Think about it; every buyer of a property in your area, will likely be a seller at some point in the future and its highly likely they also know people who are thinking of selling. Referrals are one of the ways to really help grow your agency.

This is your opportunity to sow seeds of greatness into every transaction which will give you the unfair advantage in the future once that potential client decides they want to sell. If they received great service when they bought the property, it's going to make a lasting impression so its highly likely you're the automatic choice to handle their sale when they're ready to move on. And if you did an excellent job, no other agent would get a look-in and your fees essentially become irrelevant.

However, in our experience, a lot of agents don't think long-term enough to fully take advantage of this situation and then wonder why they don't get the sale when the client is ready to move home again in the future, even though you thought you got on 'swimmingly.'

It's Easier Than It Seems

Setting yourself up for success in winning the instruction is far more intensive than just booking the appointment, doing the valuation, throwing a high marketing figure and low fee at it and crossing your fingers hoping you've won the job. You could do this of course, but your competition already are, so why not take the time to outmanoeuvre them and not only win the business, but bank a healthy fee at the same time? After all, it takes just as much effort to do a thorough job and be well-prepared as to be lackadaisical and use the shot-gun approach of playing the numbers game.

So, let's look at some of the key things you can do which will help to stack the odds in your favour to make you the automatic choice for your valuable client.

CHAPTER THREE

SECRETS OF CLIENT ASCENSION

Let's talk about one of the most interesting points about winning new business. This is what we lovingly call 'the client nurturing process' and you'll love it if you're sick and tired of seeing properties go on the market with another agent when you haven't had the chance to go and see it, or if you're fed up with your current conversion rate of valuations to new instructions, or you simply want to make more money.

The client nurturing process touches on a number of 'value-adds' to help you to achieve more from each instruction and grab higher fees. More importantly, it gives you a chance to demonstrate your expertise (and value), to potential clients in a 'non-threatening' way so they get a better feel for who you are and what you actually do for this King's ransom you'll charge them at the end of the process…

If this sounds like good news, let's dive into how the client nurturing process works…

The Old Way

Before we get too carried away with ourselves, let's look at the typical process most agents go through when it comes to valuing a property for sale. Usually, a prospective client might see an advert in the local paper or online, from a local estate agent offering something exotic called a "free valuation".

Now thinking this valuation would cost them money if they asked a surveyor to come and value it, and because they want to know how much they could achieve, the client decides to ring the estate agent to take advantage of this offer. The estate agent answers the call, takes down some details, and full of the hope of a new instruction in a desirable part of town, and with the sound of the cash register ringing in his ears, the agent rushes off to the appointment.

On the valuation, its business as usual; the valuer breezes through their presentation, carefully inserts all the little quips and stories he's told many times before, positions the conversation with the client to advise how much they feel the property is actually worth, hurriedly explains the fee they'll charge, pats the dog, comments on photos of the kids or the ones of the client's recent holiday, before leaving the property promising to follow up the appointment with a letter giving them 'a little more information' on what they'll be giving the client in exchange for their hard-earned cash.

And then the process ends as the agent scurries off to the next property, full of renewed hope that they've just bagged a new instruction, and with greater confidence, they return to the office telling everyone to expect a property coming up in that postcode in the next couple of weeks.

The shock then comes a few weeks later when the agent sees the same property advertised with a competitor at £20,000 more than he valued it at. How rude of the client! No Dear John, no phone call, no email, no nothing…

Now, for anyone paying attention, you might have realised that the number of 'touch points' the prospective client had with the agent, was two, maybe three at best:

1. The client contacted the office
2. The valuer visited the property, and
3. They received the marketing pack in the post
4. And maybe, if they're good at their job, they will have gone so far as to actually chase up the client a week or two later to see if they've decided to sell the property.

Then, after all that foreplay, the fun stops, and there's a huge anti-climax for all involved…

Failing to win the instruction, the agent blames the competition for 'overvaluing and under-feeing' the job and bemoans the unfair position of battling against two or three other local agents (who also follow the process outlined above), to try and win "a lousy instruction". Oh well, better luck next time!

Let's step back from the pity-party for a second and put ourselves into our prospective clients' high heels for a moment. She set an objective, which was to find out how much her property might be worth on the open market. Not knowing much about the moving home process, she dutifully followed the 'expert agent's' guidance of a helping hand, by calling them to take up their offer of a 'free valuation'. As she did, she noticed that not one, but all agents were offering a free valuation, and reasoning it pays to shop around for the best deal, decided to give them all the opportunity to gift her a free valuation. It's like Christmas came early!

As we detach ourselves from the emotional standpoint of being an agent, we realise all three agents in the town have taken part in a beauty parade in front of the potential client, and as they've essentially all said about the same thing, she's left with a tough choice and difficult decision to make. Who to go with..?

Yet, one very kind agent made her decision far easier by suggesting he could get more for the property than the other two, and not only would he achieve more for the property, but he would also charge less for doing so…

What a bargain!

And as the experienced agents reading this wryly smile and shake their heads in mock sympathy for the client who now falls victim to the 12-week marketing agreement tie-in, and multiple phone calls explaining how the market "has changed since they inspected the property" and "oh well, at least we tried the higher figure" or "imagine how good it would have been to get the higher figure", until its eventually reduced to the price you suggested, the point is, it's not you as the agent who's been put in the unfair position.

It's the client…

And absent the benefit of sound judgement which comes from experience (and experience generally comes from making mistakes), the client saw three people, all offering the same thing, within a similar price range, so how else could she make a decision? More to the point, how could you, as the agent, put her in this unfair position, and by doing so, stacking the odds 2:1 against you ever winning the instruction in the first place?

Aren't you meant to be protecting the clients' interests and preventing them from making a mistake that could cost them a fortune?

Now this process has been spelt out in black-and-white, some readers may be feeling uncomfortable, or downright embarrassed, as they realise what is happening day in and day out in their business. And has been happening for the last 20+ years...

Worse still, how do you then begin the quest to ask potential clients to pay more when doing so will only alienate you further from the client? When services are commoditised, as they are in the example above, there's very little a client can do to support the agent who wants to charge more. Why? Because why should they pay more when their perception is there's someone willing to achieve more for less?

The hard-hitting truth is, which no one else is going to spell out to you, no agent has truly stood out to the point where the potential client has a burning desire to work with them. And absent a compelling reason to act otherwise, the cheapest price usually wins the hearts and minds of our would-be prospects. Clearly continuing with this charade is not going to get us to where we need to be.

More to the point, where was the compelling offer to encourage the client to take action and sign up to your services?

And why wouldn't they take their time in reaching a decision if there's no scarcity around your service offering and thus no urgency created in the decision-making process to pick you over your competition?

For anyone confused by the above terms, don't worry as we'll explain more soon.

A New Way…

Now let's look at things in a different light and see what you could change if you wanted to win your prospective client's trust, so working with you is inevitable. As we work through this next section, hopefully you'll have some really cool ideas of your own.

Your prospect contacts you, as in the above example, because they saw some form of marketing designed to help them because you're offering something for free, usually a free valuation. However, when the client calls, rather than just taking details and booking the appointment, you've trained your staff to help provide the maximum value possible.

To provide this value, you use a different line of questioning aimed at finding out more about the client, and how you can serve their needs best. Let's not forget, for the uninitiated, moving home is a daunting and scary experience, one which most people haven't gone through in several years. In short, they need help! And who better to provide it, but the person they turned to in their hour of need, the forward-thinking estate agent!

During the first phone call, your crack team of staff discover they last moved home over 10 years ago, and on a scale of 1-10, with 10 being terrified, they're about an 8 on the scale when they think about how daunting this whole process might be. They also haven't yet found the right property for them, but they know they need more space. And they could also do with some input into getting the property ready for sale, because it's a little cluttered with all the children's toys.

Finally, they're thinking about using the solicitor their family has used for the last three generations (the one who you know takes six months to even read the memorandum of sale…**wishes ground would open up and swallow you whole**) but are open to recommendations.

To get all this information will require training your staff, so they can drill down into all these points during the initial call, in a way that comes across as helpful and not as an exhausting interrogation. It also involves creating some killer content (think a PDF or short video series), which the client is unlikely to find anywhere else. They especially won't find it anywhere else because it will be specifically prepared <u>by you</u>, reflecting <u>your</u> unique experience as the go-to agent in your area, giving them the best of <u>your</u> advice.

Before we jump too far ahead, be assured we'll be sharing a framework on how to do this all later in this volume. Also, don't worry that every agent reading this book is going to do exactly the same thing as you, so you'll lose your competitive edge. Most people in life will simply choose the easy way out, by preserving the status quo, even though maintaining this position is slowly killing them and their business. They reason that change is painful and risky, and who wants that? Far better to stay where they are and play it safe by doing the same as what everyone else is doing, no matter if it means their hopes and dreams are fading before their very eyes.

Anyway, back to the new way of doing things. So, after the client calls up and provides some contact details including their email address, your agency then fires over a guide on choosing the best agent to help sell their home. Now this guide is not just a pure sales pitch for your company (which is where so many agents get this wrong), but is genuine, helpful information, written as independently as possible, on how to choose the right agent to work with.

Now, let's say the appointment has been booked three, four, five or more days in advance. This suggests to the client, with careful positioning by your staff, you're so inundated with prospective clients wanting, nay **demanding**, to work with you, that it's very difficult to find time for an appointment to see their house immediately. How different does this come across to your potential client? Suddenly, there's potential 'scarcity' marketing at play, and social proof because other clients desire to work with you.

Now, instead of being a commodity and one of three random agents, you've created a situation where there's only one of you available so the prospect will be lucky if they get the opportunity to work with you. Subconsciously in the client's mind, it creates a feeling, or rather, a fear of missing out (FOMO), because they also want to work with the agent others are working with, but they may not get the opportunity to. And by sharing helpful information up front, it creates the impression that you're doing something very different to your competition.

Yet behind the scenes, you know you're just warming up, and the client is in for more surprises before you even show up at their home.

After two days, long after the client has forgotten about the call to your agency, they receive another helpful guide on what to expect from the moving home process. Recognising the client has not moved house in several years (and invariably may have had a very bad experience in the past), giving them this useful information in an easily digestible format tells them what to expect from the entire process, and how to avoid potential pitfalls, will be of significant value to them.

Already you're up to two touch points and you haven't yet been to the property. More importantly, your competition, who just dived straight in, went out to the property, ran through their standard sales pitch which provided little value, are already sat at their office with crossed fingers hoping to get the call saying they've won the business…Not so fast, the game has changed and they don't even know about it!

Two more days later, the client opens your new email leading them to a helpful video series on how to declutter their home ready for sale (in which you carefully explain why it helps them to get the best possible price), and your top tips for, quite literally, putting their house in order. So far, you've hit three of their concerns and you haven't yet set foot across the threshold!

Depending upon time constraints, either prior to, or after the appointment, you might also want to send them a very helpful and insightful guide on building their power team in preparation for their move, to include the right people such as a recommended surveyor, chosen solicitor, and preferred removals companies to work with. Now, these people may also be your preferred suppliers for some 'packaged services' which you might decide to offer as part of your renewed agency model (which we'll discuss later on in this book).

Now comes the date of the appointment. Exciting!

Not only has the client had at least two-to-three more touch points in the form of the very helpful information (which no other agent has provided), suddenly you're entering the property as a, nay THE, perceived expert in your field (remember, perception is reality).

Particularly though video content, the client will have already started to build a subconscious bond with you, creating an unspoken desire to work with you.

Note, your competitors will not have created this same desire because they're simply turning up on the day to breeze through the same presentation they've run a gazillion times, yet wholly unprepared to face the client who has now been carefully warmed up by your superior marketing skills and expert guidance on what matters most to them.

You also now have additional talking points at the appointment, which allows further opportunities to demonstrate your expert knowledge, to show you really are the preferred agent to work with. You've already warmed the prospect up to who you are and what you do, which is helpful when a client suggests your competitors will do the job for less. You can merely ask the client whether the competition have given similar in-depth information you've provided? Chances are they won't have, and certainly not to the extent you have if you've embraced this process fully.

Hopefully you can already see the angle here which dictates you're clearly worth the increased fee you're about to quote… ;-)

Finally, let's say you choose not to do anything different during your appointment other than suggest there's several clients in the pipeline who want to work with you, and you only have capacity to take on a small number of clients at any one time. This week, you have space to take on two more clients, and you've already got five other appointments booked with seriously interested sellers. If they don't want one, it's not a problem for them to say no, but you're just making them aware of the situation, so they don't miss out, if they did want to work with you. There's nothing worse than starting a relationship off on the wrong foot because a client cannot work with you for several weeks because you're already serving others who were faster decision makers…

Psychologically, this reverses the balance of power away from the client and leaves them with the possibility of working with a lesser agent if they don't quickly make the decision to work with you. Suddenly, the choice they must make is not one of three, but one of one, and they'd better make it quick if they want to secure your expertise and professionalism. The client is now in a position where they may experience FOMO, and as such, their desire to work with you will automatically increase.

This is a very difficult situation for most estate agents to get their head around when they have had years of being ground down by the constant dogfight of trying to secure as many instructions as possible at what is effectively a break-even fee level. And it's usually at the expense of making themselves available to their clients 24/7, to the exclusion of family events and their private lives. To contemplate turning down instructions because you 'couldn't fit them into your current workload' is a situation most agents would think is unbearable.

More is always better, right? Well, not exactly…

Because the client only has a very limited opportunity to work with you, not only does this increase your desirability, but also helps you increase your fees. You're clearly in demand (after all, none of the other agents said this to them), and you've already demonstrated your expertise up to this point.

Not only have you increased the clients desire to work with you, you may even be able to get them to sign your agreement there and then, at the higher fee. And all because you decided to stop doing what everyone else is doing, take a step back, create a few valuable resources which will really help your clients (and which you can use quite literally forever!), and not work yourself into an early grave by being available at all times of the day and night for clients who only want to pay less than 1%.

You could even go one step further and pull out the 'Ultimate Authority Builder' (see Volume III – if you haven't got that yet go to– http://www.wiggywam.co.uk/estateagentssecretstrilogy to grab it whilst you remember!) which you hand to your client as a thank you gift for inviting you into their home. This handy little instruction winner initiates the psychology of reciprocity where your client will not only be impressed with your work but will also want to return the favour by giving you the instruction.

Finally, instead of going into a 'head-to-head take-it-or-leave-it' situation over your fees, you instead offer your client a menu of services structured in differently priced packages which they get to choose from to match their needs. Are they a 'no-frills just give me the basics kinda client', or do they want the full red carpet Rolls Royce treatment? All being well, you've taken the time to design packages for both ends of the scale as well as the middle!

The good news is, it doesn't stop there. Let's suggest, regardless of whether you won the instruction or not, once you get back to the office, you not only send them your normal marketing report, but you also place them into a fully automated future client nurturing process. This might mean sharing a few helpful videos over the course of the next few weeks which expand on information you shared during your appointment, and which will be helpful in their upcoming move.

These videos might include an interview with a removal's expert for example, where they share some top tips on getting your removals booked in at the best possible price, and how to make the physical moving process easy. This might seem like an insignificant point, until we consider most people have lived in a house for 5+ years and have accumulated an awful lot of stuff. Surely a good de-clutter before they put their home up for sale can only be a good thing.

Then you might provide a series of training videos which help your prospect to understand the whole process of moving home (expanding on your PDF content), and why you're the best agent to work with because you've demonstrated more of your expertise. If this includes video testimonials from past clients who were happy with your service, this gives the client further confidence they've made the right choice to work with you.

By now, you can see we've gone from a previous average 3-4 touch points, to having 10-15+, with helpful information provided to your client without pushy sales tactics and without needing to railroad them into signing the marketing agreement because you need to meet your targets! Using the benefit of technology allows you to automate all of this and do many things on top of the basics of texting or emailing the client reminders about your appointment.

You may even decide to send a personalised, handwritten greeting card, thanking them for the opportunity to view their home and letting them know how much you're looking forward to working with them. These little touches show the client you're in a class of your own. We're sure you can start thinking of many other ideas to include in your marketing process to win a client's trust and bag more instructions than ever before. Doing the things your competition won't do, will truly help to build your profile, increase your perceived value, and give you plenty of room to increase your fees.

Multiple Touch Points

When you start the work of creating more touch points with prospective clients, it's helpful to go through the moving home process in fine detail to work out what the obstacles your prospect will likely face. Most agents wrongly assume clients just want to sell their home and move, but this simplistic stance overlooks multiple potential problems and objectives they may be trying to achieve at the same time.

For example, does your prospect want to move home to get their child into a certain school? This is a more common reason than most agents perhaps realise. What if you provided a guide detailing exactly how to stand the best possible chance of securing a place in that particular school? Would any of the agents in your area provide such value? Would it take much work to go and interview the school about their admissions process and what the school is looking for when they accept new students into their ranks? Or for the lazy amongst us, visiting the school's website and rejigging their admission process into a user-friendly guide...?

Once your information products have been made, they're pretty much done for life, yet the return on time invested in these marketing materials is significant. Best of all, you may be able to outsource some or all this work to a virtual assistant on Upwork or Fiverr who could help compile some of them at relatively low cost.

The only question is, how badly do you want this? The motivated and committed will find a way. The 'wantrepreneurs' will see this as a good idea, but fail to take enough action to make it a reality.

Giving Maximum Value

To get maximum value from this process, it's helpful to sit down with a blank piece of paper and write at the top; "what potential problems do my clients face when it comes to moving home?" Then list every single point, problem, or frustration your clients might face.

Why bother? After all, the system is what it is and everyone has to go through it, right? Firstly, your client won't know many of the obstacles they'll face without some prior warning from an expert in the field (you). Secondly, you get paid most when you solve problems for others. That's literally what your client will pay handsomely for.

Sure, they know they want to move home, but do they know the solicitor they're thinking of using has an average transaction time of five eons and if they go with them, there's a chance they won't meet their timeline to get little Harry into Hogwart's school? This is the sort of advice they need, but more importantly, will pay you well for if you can help make their dreams a reality. So, put the whole process under a microscope and list all the problems, obstacles, concerns or worries your experience has shown matter most to your clients.

Look at the many different frustrations a client may be faced with, such as how do they choose the right solicitor or how do they choose the right surveyor? Will they get ripped off by their estate agent? Will they lose the house of their dreams if they can't sell quickly enough? How do they go about navigating the mortgage market and get the right advice from whole-of-market brokers? How do they achieve maximum value from the sale of their property? What should they do when it comes to people viewing the property? Are they confident enough to show people round their home on their own or should they seek professional help? And just how do they negotiate the best deal on the home of their dreams? Can anyone help them with this?

The answers to some of these questions may seem incredibly basic to an estate agent with 15-20+ years' experience, but we must keep coming back to the fact that your client has not moved home in several years and perhaps the last time they did, it was fraught with frustration. More importantly, this is actually what you're selling – your expertise in helping them manage this transition, not the standard "we put all of our properties online and the best way to keep up to date is to look there, or get on our mailing list" …

By doing this exercise, you're presenting yourself with multiple opportunities to help your client and get paid the rewards you deeply deserve! Do some of the challenges seem too big? Work on solving the little ones and work towards the bigger ones. Some may require the cooperation of others so as you build your power team and try different things, you'll eventually find the goldmine you've been searching for.

So, continue working through your list, highlighting the pitfalls, traps or concerns your client may have to face and how you, as the expert in your local area, can help be their guide. If you're struggling for inspiration at this point, simply review several the most recent valuations you've attended and recall some of the key questions repeated by your prospective clients.

If you're serious about making more money from your agency, it's important not to skip this exercise, because it truly is the best way to show how you can move your business from being a commodity, towards being a one-of-a-kind, for which you can charge outstanding fees for being the most desirable agent to work with.

The Solutions List

Once you've gone through the list of problems your clients might face (BIG HINT – we covered a lot of them in Volume I – can you see the structure we've used now?), the next thing we need to do is work out all the possible solutions our clients would benefit from. So, grab a fresh sheet of paper and write out all the potential solutions your clients might use.

The quickest and easiest way to do this is to take your list of problems and start writing out possible solutions. Coming back to the example of choosing the right solicitor, could you provide them with a guide called "The simple how-to guide on choosing the right solicitor"? To compile the guide, you might interview a couple of local solicitors in your area who you refer work to and who would be willing to join you on a Zoom call to discuss the top things they consider essential when it comes to choosing a solicitor.

Doing this exercise can offer multiple possible solutions, so it's vital you don't sensor yourself, no matter how wacky or wild your ideas might be! This list will become more and more valuable as time goes on and you transition through the next stages of the process. What you're doing is compiling a huge arsenal of resources so you have one to solve literally every single problem a client might be facing. Can you see how powerful this is? Not only is it a clear demonstration you know exactly what you're talking about, you'll highlight the success a client can achieve by working with you because you know all the potential obstacles they'll face, AND you have all the possible solutions.

Now we have a complete list of all the solutions to their problems, we now need to look at how we can deliver these solutions to our client. So, grab another sheet of paper and start to work through the next list.

Methods Of Delivery

When considering methods of delivery for these solutions, it's likely, at least initially, you'll have limited resources to start implementing. Providing a premium service requires clients to pay premium fees (think Selling Sunset), and if you want to increase profits in your business, you must have a significant margin between the <u>price you're charging</u> to deliver the service and the <u>cost to fulfil it</u>.

Ideally, you want to increase the difference between the two as much as possible so you can make your business wildly profitable. The only realistic way to do this is to employ technology and a rinse-and-repeat model. What we mean is you're going to do the work once to provide value forever to all your prospects, and then use technology to put this information in front of your client in a way which encourages them to take action quickly and invest in your services.

The key to implementing your solutions is to take each solution on your list, and then write out all the different methods of delivery you could use. As an example, you might want to deliver some content via a simple PDF. For other content, it might be appropriate to use video, a structured training format, or a recorded Zoom call with an expert in their field. Or you might decide to invite clients to a private Q&A webinar, or small informal gathering at a local hotel to go through changes in landlord legislation for example. Yet other solutions might need you to work closely with chosen expert experts in your local area to deliver huge value in a way your competition cannot possibly achieve via the use of packaged services of work.

By using technology as much as possible, it effectively allows you to have an army of digital robots delivering a high level of service to potential clients no matter the time of day or night. As you get better at working through this process, you can simply add clients into your client nurturing program and let technology take care of the rest. You then just deal with any enquiries or questions they may have as they come in via phone, text, or email.

Your Personal Touch

When you've considered the different levels of service you want to provide to your client, you want to work out what level of personal involvement you want to give your clients and contrast this against the level of effort expected from them to achieve their desired result.

Hopefully by now, you can see the fantastic opportunity to offer different levels of service based on the amount of work expected from the client. Most people will want to take the easiest route possible to achieve their desired result. This allows you to offer a few different options (at different price points), to your clients to help them achieve their goal.

For example, when someone wants to renovate their bathroom, they have the following options:

1. Go down the DIY route. This might be cheaper if they have the skills to do it but requires a significant time commitment from them to get the bathroom replaced as quickly as possible.

2. Pay somebody else to come in and do the work for them. This may increase costs but hopefully means results will be better and quicker, without the stress and hassle they might otherwise experience trying to do it all on their own.

Looking at the different levels of service you could potentially provide, your clients will have to go and find several different people to work with in the whole process, such as mortgage brokers, surveyors, solicitors etc. However, you may have a power team the client could plug into straight away. However, most agents undervalue themselves and give away these key contacts for free because they want to be liked and they think this is the quickest way to win business. Yet this is false economy because when you start to understand all the value you have to offer, you'll realise what you're doing has significant value to your clients over and above the cash value they pay you in exchange.

For example, working with the right solicitor could save them hundreds of hours of stress, worry, and frustration as they go through the buying and selling process. If you asked your client if they would willingly pay a slightly higher price for conveyancing to avoid hundreds of hours of stress, uncertainty, and sleepless nights, if you've educated them about why this is important, they would invariably say "yes". This now opens the door to offering different packaged services to your client which is exciting!

If you usually charge 1.5% to sell a client's home, and a professional solicitor would cost £1,500+ for conveyancing, you could package both up, at say 2% fee depending on property value. Working this way makes the client's job of buying your services so much easier because you're taking a lot of the decisions, frustrations, and stress away from them, whilst securing the very best people to work with. You should not underestimate how important this is to them. And you.

The 10X To $1/10^{th}$ Test

This is something we learned from a marketing mentor called Alex Hormozi, who is an expert at showing people how to create additional value for their clients. The 10X to one-tenth test stretches your mind to consider many different ways to deliver the different levels of service you're considering offering to your chosen clients.

To do this effectively, the question you should ask is; "If our clients were to pay us 10 times the current price they pay right now, what level of service could we provide?"

Now before you switch off and think there's no way a client would pay you 10% commission to sell their home, just remember in some parts of the world, real estate agents are regularly charging 5 to 8%. That's 500-800% greater than what most UK agents achieve.

Start to use your creative brain power to think about how you could employ this in your business, so if a client were to pay you a 10% fee, what could you possibly provide as a level of service to help them achieve their end goal? Such a significant fee should give you capacity to offer a completely different level of service and give you ideas on how to further distinguish yourself from your competition.

For example, you could provide an all-inclusive package, where you provide the surveying services, the mortgage broking services, the solicitor's fees, removals, and your most advanced standard of service as an all-in-one package.

You could also offer a service where you go and look at the home they're thinking about buying, and give them expert feedback based on your years of experience, about their future home. You might also want to take this a step further and shoulder the responsibility of negotiating the price of their new home to help demonstrate as much value as possible. This becomes even more exciting because you could negotiate a performance related fee based on the level of discount you achieve for them, i.e., you get 10% of every £1,000 you save them off the purchase price.

Is this all starting to look a bit different to the traditional way of doing things?

Who's excited?!

Now, once you've looked at all the different areas where you could offer a 10X service level to your client, the next step is to ask yourself; "If a client were to pay us $1/10^{th}$ of the price we're currently charging, what services would we be able to provide within that price constraint?"

Wait! Before you go crazy thinking we've defaulted on our promises to help you make more money by offering your services for 0.1%, and there's no way you're going to work for a pittance, the point of this exercise is to stretch your mind in the other direction and look at how you could offer greater service to your potential clients in ways that cost you precious little.

It broadens your mind on the different ways you can help your clients achieve the same results but for far less investment from them. This literally forces you to look specifically at automating certain aspects of your service, so you can deliver it to them for far less cost.

For example, you might decide to deal solely with all their enquiries via an online messaging service, email, or text message rather than in-person enquiries. You might decide to sell paid-for information products which give significant value for the price a client pays, or even teach them a Do-It-

Yourself method of selling their home on their own. They're literally just paying you for information within a PDF or eBook on how to sell their home themselves and there may be a market for this. It might seem like a difficult exercise to do, but hopefully it'll expand your mind in such a way you start to get creative with the possible solutions you could provide.

This might seem like a conflict as we talked about just wanting to increase our fees throughout the book so far, however the whole point of this exercise is to give you as many weapons in your arsenal which you can use to outperform your competition. You'll see how useful these ideas are when it comes to packaging up your services later on in this book. Writing them down doesn't mean you're actually going to do them; you're just coming up with ideas at this stage. All will become clear shortly!

If you want to know how you can really add value to your clients and your business, there's a ton of extra resources we can share with you on a call.

We just ask you to invest 30 minutes into a complimentary consultation, where we can help fast-track your success (with no hard sell whatsoever).

Here's the link to book your call:

http://www.wiggywam.co.uk/estateagentssecretscall

CHAPTER FOUR

SECRETS OF SETTING YOURSELF UP
FOR SUCCESS

You've heard it before. If you fail to plan, then you plan to fail.

The time and effort you put into doing some groundwork before attending the property to give a valuation or market appraisal can pay dividends. Incidentally, we know a lot of agents call the valuation appointment by a lot of different names, but for our purposes, we'll call it a valuation.

You want to do your research before you're on site and be armed with as much data and information as possible. How much research have you done on the property before you get there? When was it last sold? How much did it sell for? Which agent sold it? Has it been extended or redeveloped in any way since it was last sold? Is the seller on your mailing list looking for other properties in the area? If so, how many times have you contacted them? Have they been kept up to date with all properties that came to the market which meet their requirements? How much nurturing of this potential client have you done?

There's usually a discrepancy between the service agents <u>think</u> they give clients on their mailing list <u>and the service they actually receive</u>. The answers to some of these questions may shock you and be wildly different to what you thought your automated mailing list was doing. Still, it's better to know than be in the dark as the answers to these questions will give you a plan of action.

As we saw earlier, your staff booking the appointment should aim to take down as much information as possible from the prospective client, yet without being too intrusive. It's always worth politely asking on the phone why they're looking to sell and if they've found a property they want to move to. You'll be asking these questions when you're on the appointment anyway, but the point is, you'll be able to compare answers to see if they're genuine with their enquiry or not.

Gathering as much information as possible when booking the appointment will not only help you to feel informed and to start building rapport with the client, but you'll also be able to plan enough time into your diary to carry out the inspection based on their personality type and needs. If there's one thing that's common with a lot of agents, its they're always late, and the most common cause of this is not enough time being planned into the diary for the valuer to make it from one appointment to the next. This looks tardy and puts you under pressure before you've even arrived at the appointment. Can you imagine a Rolls-Royce salesman acting in the same way?

A word of warning: iPads and tablets are great but keep as much information as you can in paper format so that can provide it as tangible evidence during the appointment. This is especially true when it comes to positioning your valuation by ensuring you're providing your client with a realistic figure, benchmarked against other comparables in your area.

The Valuation Consultation

The valuation appointment provides you with a great opportunity to build rapport with your client, so they know, like, and trust you. People **only** do business with people they know, like and trust. So, if you can get to this point with the seller during the appointment (or even better, before the appointment due to your client nurturing process), you're more than likely going to win the business.

We all know how hard it is to say 'no' to a friend, so we want to try and build a friendship during our inspection, by matching their personality type to such an extent that you're the obvious choice for them to do business with and nobody else gets a look-in!

Now here's a little secret we want to share with you that most agents overlook to their detriment. They've been hoodwinked to think that salespeople must be fast-talking, obtuse and constantly trying to get the client to sign on the dotted line immediately. Picture any movie involving a salesperson and you'll immediately conjure up the same image of an aggressive salesman who thinks "coffee is for closers" and who is constantly pushing for the business whilst undermining their client with aggressive sales tactics to the point of insult until their client relents and just signs!

But what does that do to your client? Does it make them want to do business with you to the exclusion of all others? Or does it get their back up so they can't wait to get you out of their home? For most, it's the latter, and pushy agents don't realise the damage they're doing to their business trying to emulate some character from the movie Glengarry Glenross!

Who Are The Best Salespeople?

Think about this for a second.

Who are the best salespeople in the world? Car salesmen? How about the person who runs the local ice-cream van? Yes, that's the one! Who can resist delicious ice-cream? Especially on a hot summer's day! But don't you find they always seem to drive off at the exact moment you've grabbed your cash and run out the door?

Nope, it's not any of them!

A Rolls-Royce salesperson you say? Ah, we can see where you're going with this. But nope.

The best salespeople you will meet are quiet, unassuming and technically not salespeople, but they are ruthlessly effective, nonetheless. Who are they?

Doctors.

That's right. Doctors. How, you may ask? Well, think about it. When you go to visit a doctor for whatever reason, do they immediately write you a prescription the moment you walk through the door? And what would you think of them if they did? Wouldn't you want to see them struck off?

No, they don't do any of that. You sit down, and they start a **consultation process** with you.

They ask questions. They drill down for information to help diagnose the issue before they make a recommendation. To do otherwise puts them in the position of being guilty of malpractice and they could be struck off.

Yet, when a doctor makes a recommendation, people invariably follow it. Why? Well, think about it. They've taken the time to understand the problem. They've gone through some questions with you to diagnose the issue. They've taken an interest in you as a person and perhaps run some tests. They've also studied hard and carry some authority, professionalism, and gravitas with their degree on the wall and white cape.

Most importantly, they asked questions and then **listened!** Add to that the fact that you were likely in some sort of pain, and you wanted immediate relief.

So, when they make a recommendation, most people usually follow it.

How Does This Apply To Estate Agency?

Think about how you approach the selling of your services compared to a doctor. Do you dive right in and make a recommendation to them without giving them the time of day to understand their situation? Or do you think you would be perceived as far more professional if you took the time to carefully question the seller, understand their situation, build rapport with them, find out their why and demonstrate how you can help them achieve their goals, dreams, and objectives?

Or would it be better to waltz in, dash around the property, overvalue it, under-fee it and cross your fingers in the hope that you'll win the job, because after all, getting to 'yes' is just a numbers game taught by all the half-baked sales trainers out there and you're already half an hour late for your next appointment!

We respectfully suggest it depends on how you want to run your business and whether you want to be a 'stack-'em-high-and-sell-'em-cheap' agent or if you want to be a professional agent who gets paid handsomely for the exclusive and higher perceived value service they provide to their clients.

If you want to sell like a doctor, run your client through a series of questions to find their motivation and reasons for selling, their history with the property, and who they are as a person. Write the answers down and be seen to be doing so. Take a genuine interest in what they're saying by carefully listening and expanding on the answers they give you. Ultimately, you want to make your client feel heard. This is a consultation, not a monologue!

(If you're not familiar with the term 'feeling heard', think about a time when you sat down to open up to someone about something personal that was bothering you, and just as you got to a sensitive part of your story, they cut across you or were insensitive in some way which stopped you dead in your tracks and made you reluctant to share more. That's not feeling heard. A more sensitive person, counsellor, or good friend, will patiently take an interest in the person sharing, listen to them, ask questions, even take notes to refer back to and talk about their own similar life experiences, AFTER the person has finished explaining themselves. Do not underestimate the power of this; when people begin to open up like this, and they do because selling a home is a very personal thing, follow this guidance and you'll find people are drawn to you in a way that most find difficult to comprehend).

You'll come back to the notes that you've written down later. Their own words, observations, and comments can be excellent tools to use when it comes to tipping the balance in your favour to win the instruction, and at a fee that's worth a lot to you. It's very difficult to argue against words that have come out of your own mouth!

The Golden Rule Of All Business

"All things being equal, people will do business with, and refer business to, those people they know, like and trust" – Bob Burg

Commit this to memory, and practice attaining the wisdom embedded within it, and you will not go far wrong.

CHAPTER FIVE

THE SECRET CONSULTATION ROADMAP

Let's go through an overview of the valuation consultation process so you can see how this fits together when it comes to getting your client to know, like and trust you.

When entering the property, you should first sit down with the client to start building rapport through an informal conversation. Invariably your client will ask you where you want to start. You can start off by saying something along the lines of the following:

"We usually start by asking a few quick questions, so do you mind if we sit down first of all just to run through them?"

Invariably they will agree to your request, and this is a very 'non-threatening' way of starting an appointment. They will usually offer to make you a drink so you should always accept if you want to build rapport. There's nothing better to assist in connecting with someone in a non-threatening manner than an informal chat over a nice hot drink. Sitting down in a comfortable environment and running through a few questions will help your potential client feel at ease and give the perception that you're professional and thorough in your approach.

Incidentally, if you're visiting a home that would be ideal material for 'filthy house SOS' or other similar TV program, it's best to accept their hospitality by simply asking for a glass of water, pretending to take a sip, and then leaving it on the side. They won't take offence to this, where they might if you've refused a cup of tea, or they made you one and you didn't drink it because you couldn't quite work out if they've made it from the kettle or the hot tap! And when did they last clean that cup…?

One memory is attending an appointment once at a beautiful country home owned by a nice old lady. We sat in the garden as she poured the coffee and offered us cream. Our colleague politely accepted. Just then we noticed its lumpy texture and quickly declined but found mild amusement watching the grimaces on his face as he drank the sour cream coffee so as not to offend the homeowner and lose the instruction!

Start with a blank sheet of paper and write the client's name(s) on the top of the sheet. Double-check the spelling of the client's name as its embarrassing when you get it wrong because you can't read your colleagues handwriting...

Ask the client two opening questions to get the consultation started:

1. What are they hoping to achieve from the sale of their property?
2. What are their expectations from the agent handling the sale?

Do these questions seem complicated? No, but they will reveal a lot about a client's assumptions, what they hope to achieve, and their expectations of **you**. One of the biggest breakdowns in communication is when two parties have different (uncommunicated) expectations about the outcome of the same situation. This happens often when people assume things.

And do you know what happens when you assume things?

You make an ass out of u and me...

Assumptions are deadly, can lead to miscommunications, and the loss of business to any competitor who takes the time to ask questions and drills down a little deeper so they can better understand their prospective client's motivations.

As George Bernard Shaw once said: "The biggest problem with communication is the illusion it has taken place".

So, always ask questions. And if you're not sure, ask some more questions! Just try not to do it in a way that feels like an interrogation or whilst shining a spotlight in their face! That's why you sit down comfortably, over a hot drink and take notes whilst they're giving you answers to your questions. There's a fine art between understanding your client's objectives and building rapport with them, to making your client feel like they're facing the Spanish inquisition!

If something's not clear, you should always say something like; "For clarity…" or "Just so we can be clear…" or "Just so I can make sure I have understood you correctly, is this an accurate summary of what you've just said…" and repeat back to them what they just said. Only when you are clear do you have a good chance of knowing and understanding your client.

Ask questions. Take notes. Simple.

Personality Profiling

We covered this in Volume I, but make no mistake about it, personality profiling can be the key to winning the instruction. Most agents will be at least broadly familiar with personality profiling and the need to 'mix and match' your personality style with your potential client, so they subconsciously build some form of a bond with you.

However, in our experience, a lot of agents fail to understand this adequately, and so set themselves up to lose as much as 75-80% of business as a result. Make a mental note of their personality style whilst you're talking to them, so you can conduct yourself and relay information to them in a way which they find most appealing.

The Property Inspection

Now, each agent will have their own way of doing things when it comes to looking round the property. That's not something we want to tell you how to do. Our own preference was to look around the inside of the property, starting on the ground floor, then head upstairs, before going outside to look at the externals. By doing it this way and looking around the outside last of all, it gave a few minutes to review notes and nail down a figure for the valuation before heading back inside to discuss it with the homeowner. But do what works best for you.

One secret tip we can offer is, it's worth spending a little longer at the property taking similar notes which you would take were you to win the instruction and list the property for sale. The first advantage is that it gives you a psychological edge as you're already acting as if the client is going to list their property with you. The second is that it saves a lot of time when writing up sales particulars which you can more than likely do from your notes without having to revisit the property. This is especially useful if your agency employs external resources to do photographs and floor plans so you can get started the moment the client gives you instructions. And let them know you can do this for them.

Delivering The Valuation

The biggest stumbling blocks agents face when delivering their pitch relate to their valuation of the property, and the fee they'd charge for selling it.

It's like the agent must climb a mountain with twin peaks; the first summit they have to scale is delivering the marketing figure that's in line with the client's expectations, (so they don't upset them and automatically put themselves on the back foot), and the second is presenting the fee in a way the service package sits well with them.

The hurdle an agent must clear in making these successful summits is usually the agent's competition – what did they value the property at and what fee are they offering to charge? Both of those are the biggest mental roadblocks for most agents.

Why?

Well, simply because experience appears to have taught them that the agent who overvalues and underfees the job is the one that walks away with it. After they've tied the poor client into a 12 week (or indefinite), marketing agreement and gone through several rounds of; "I'm sorry Mr/s client, the market's slower than it was, so perhaps it's time to reduce the price of the property…" to eventually get the property down to the level you valued it at, but it's now been sold by your competition, and they pocket the fee.

Have faith friends; there is another way! We've already touched on the perception of value earlier in this handbook, however the road to successfully winning an instruction can be made a lot easier with the support of some facts and figures. Always remember, your client is not an idiot, and for the one in ten clients who may behave in a manner that makes you think otherwise, 90% market share is good enough for you to build a strong business!

So, let's look at how we can kick your competition in the pants and win the job (at a healthy fee).

Setting Up The Consultation

This is where we sort the wheat from the chaff. The set-up of this part of the process can be instrumental in you winning the business and overcoming objections before they even enter your client's head. For brevity, we've bullet-pointed some of the things you want to consider to make your presentations successful:

- **Aim to have no distractions** – this includes your phone going off during the presentation/pitch. Ensure, so far as possible, that you cannot be disturbed. If the house is very busy and you cannot steal enough time in peace and quiet to talk directly to the decision makers, it may pay you to remove yourself and then invite them into your office for a coffee to talk further and conduct your pitch in a more controlled environment. If your client is distracted, they won't take into account what you're saying, and you can't serve them to the best of your ability. Moving the game to your home turf might just give you the competitive advantage, particularly if there are screaming kids running around!

- **Positioning** - Always sit next to or adjacent to your prospect, rather than opposite them. Sitting opposite can lead to confrontation by adopting physically opposing positions against one another. Sitting next to your client is less confrontational and physically demonstrates you're on their side. It also removes any barriers between you and your client (such as a table) and makes a more comfortable environment for the client to open up to you. Just be careful not to sit too close if they've only got a two-seater sofa...that might be a bit awkward!

- **Pitching** - If you're speaking to more than one person, sit them both next to each other so that your head isn't bobbing back and forth as though you're watching a tennis match! By sitting the parties you're talking to next to one other, your eye contact isn't far away from them, and you can see their reactions as you talk. Subtleties in body-language and facial expression can alert you to potential roadblocks and help you overcome hurdles the moment you see them happen.

- **Information** – Before you lead into your pitch, you want to be armed with the information you gathered before you arrived at the property. This will help guide your potential clients clearly through your presentation so they can see where you're coming from. The paper-based comparables will help to give your clients <u>tangible</u> examples of properties which are similar to theirs that they can see, touch and relate to, rather than the presentation given by your competition using the P.F.A. method of valuation (Pluck From Air)!

- **Listen intently but speak with authority** – Clients do sometimes need to be told what to do. You need to have certainty about you and tell them what they need to do. Always look them in the eye when you're advising them. Always be looking for clues in what your prospect is saying to you. Ask them: "How can we help you move forward?" and listen intently to their answer. Look out for their pain points (things they need to change or move away from). Continuously reinforce: "This is the right decision for you because....." and tell them why you believe it's right for them and is in alignment with their goals and any pain points they've identified they want to move away from.

- **Use language that drives the sale** - For example, NEVER SAY;
  o Fee – instead say, "investment"
  o Sell – instead say, "we get our clients involved"
  o Contract – instead say, "paperwork"
  o Sign – instead say, "ok, authorise, approve"
  o Customers – instead say, "people we serve" or "our valued clients"
  o Cheapest – instead say, "most economical"

    o   Problems – instead say "challenges" or optimistically, "opportunities"

Now your clients are sat adjacent to you, and you're armed with the right information to deliver your pitch, relax, and have some fun. You've also got, both in the back of your mind and on your notepad in front of you, your client's motivations, hopes and aspirations which are going to come in handy as you progress through this next part of the process. They'll also come in handy when you encounter any objections raised and how you can use your expert guidance to help them achieve their needs and wants.

[As an aside, assuming you win the instruction (or even if you don't), these pain points can be used by you and your staff in the office in helping to tip the balance in your client's favour to get an offer accepted, sell them another property, or win them back if they initially instructed another agent. They're also amazing sources of inspiration for information products for your customer nurturing journey].

If you want to know how you can really add value to your clients and your business, there's a ton of extra resources we can share with you on a call.

We just ask you to invest 30 minutes into a complimentary consultation, where we can help fast-track your success (with no hard sell whatsoever).

Here's the link to book your call:

        http://www.wiggywam.co.uk/estateagentssecretscall

CHAPTER SIX

SECRETS TO PRESENT YOUR ESTIMATION OF VALUE

The first thing we want you to consider is this: You may not be right. Odd thing to open with? Well, not exactly. We all have off-days. We all make mistakes. We all get things wrong. And so, it's important not to be too attached to the outcome. You're going to give it your best shot and you're going to be as professional as possible, so if that's not enough, then so be it. Relax, and have fun!

When it comes to presenting your estimate of value, as a professional, you're not just going to blurt out some figure you've just plucked from thin air like an amateur. You're going to guide your client down a sensible road to reach a figure you're happy to market the property at. Here's how we would approach it:

"Now, Mr/s Client, your home is an excellent example of a four-bedroom, modern detached house which I know is going to appeal to a lot of potential buyers. However, I'm sure you will agree, it's important that your property is priced sensibly for a number of reasons, not least of all because marketing it at too high a price can put people off looking, and that's the last thing we want to do, because failing to secure you a buyer early enough in the process could mean you miss out on the home of your dreams. Secondly, properties that are overvalued tend to stick around on the market for a long time so prospective buyers then start asking the question; 'what's wrong with it'. I'm sure you're keen to avoid both scenarios…"

Get their agreement.

"Great, it's good to know we are on the same page! Ok, so when we appraise a property for marketing purposes, to do it accurately, rather than doing the P.F.A. approach (you can make a joke out of this), we look to what we call 'comparables' in the local area as a reasonable estimate of value. This is vitally important because it's essentially the same job a surveyor will have to do when they come and value the property for the buyer's mortgage. If your marketing price is too high, even if a potential buyer might initially agree to pay it, if the surveyor then says it's not worth it, you'll lose out because the buyer will renegotiate the price, or worse, pull out altogether! This could mean you've lost money on professional legal fees or again, lose the home of your dreams. Incidentally, last year alone, this exact scenario cost British homeowners just shy of £1 Billion in lost fees, or approximately £1,800 each when a deal falls through. I'm sure you're keen to avoid that scenario aren't you…?"

Again, get their agreement.

"I can see that you're exactly the kind of sensible client's we like to work with and you're clearly not going to be swayed by some 'pie in the sky' appraisal. You want hard facts to base your important decision upon, don't you?

Get their agreement.

"Great! And we'd like to give those to you. So, looking at the first comparable; this is a property which we sold recently not far from here. As you can see, it's a 3-bedroom detached property of a similar age and condition and we sold that one for £360,000. Now clearly your property, being a four bedroomed home is going to be worth more than that, wouldn't you agree…?"

Again, get their agreement. Everybody always thinks that their house is worth more! What we're doing here is giving a foundation for your appraisal to sit on. Some clients do not realise how much the market has moved on and if they've been in their home for a long time, they may be shocked as to the actual valuation you give them. We're also building up our number of 'yes's' from the client; a very important concept in the psychology of sales. After a strong string of yes's, it's more difficult for someone to say no.

"Great. So, clearly, we would expect to get more than £360,000 for your home. Our next comparable here is a 5-bedroom detached property that sold just last month to cash buyers very quickly. You can see that not only does it have an extra bedroom, but it also has a double garage and two en-suite bathrooms. This property sold very quickly at £440,000. Taking that one into account, and as I know you're sensible clients, clearly, we wouldn't expect to be marketing your property at close to this figure as they're two very different animals. Wouldn't you agree?

Again, get their agreement. Depending upon what (false) expectations may have been planted in their minds by another agent, this is where you might encounter some resistance. If the P.F.A. approach from another agent has put a much higher figure in their mind, this approach helps to bring them back to reality.

Without getting into too much back-and-forth and positionality of "I'm right, you're wrong" with the client, if they do start to raise objections with you at this point concerning the appraised value, then you can enquire where they got that figure from. If it's from your competition, ask if the agent concerned has shown them true and accurate comparable evidence. Again, tell them that the surveyor down valuing the property is your biggest concern because you don't want to lead them into false expectations or be the agent responsible for costing them money if this happens. And again, warn them of the consequences of losing their dream home if they can't proceed or costing themselves over £1,800 in abortive fees if their buyer pulls out.

What you also need to bear in mind at this point is simple rational expectations. If the client has wholly unrealistic expectations, do not be afraid let them go. Research from Rightmove suggests 35-40% of all house sales are successfully achieved only after a change of estate agent. So, let your competition waste their money advertising it at the higher price. When you know you're right, let them prove how foolish they are whilst you keep nurturing the client throughout the duration of their marketing agreement, ready to pounce on them once they've realised you were right all along.

Now, assuming they're in agreement with you and the second comparable is a much better property than theirs, this is where you go in for the kill. Your third comparable should be as close to their property as possible so they can see you're fairly valuing their home against what the market is willing to pay.

So, you'd say something along the lines of; "Great. So, clearly, we would not expect to get £440,000 for your home and I am pleased to see that you're realistic in your approach to marketing your property. Our third and final comparable here is a very similar 4 bedroom detached property which sold two months ago. You can see that it's identical in almost every respect and therefore is an excellent comparable for reference. This property sold at £390,000 and that figure was endorsed by the buyer's valuation surveyor who was happy to confirm it as a realistic sale price. This gives us a very healthy guide and I would expect you to achieve a very similar figure once we've run our marketing campaign for the property. How does that sound to you?"

Now that the 'first hurdle' of the presentation or first peak of the mountain has been scaled, sit back and listen to your client's reactions with enthusiasm. Listen to what they have to say. Do they agree with you? Do they think that figure is fair? Did they expect a higher figure or a lower one? Do they have any objections whatsoever as far as the price is concerned and what are their motivations for saying what they're saying to you?

Write down their objections and make sure they've aired all thoughts they may have before you go on to tackle them. Do not interrupt their flow to answer as each objection is raised; just take notes. The only thing you should be asking at this point is "Ok, is there anything else that concerns you about the valuation we've suggested?" Encourage them to get everything off their chest so you can tackle all those objections as you head into the second hurdle, or second peak of the mountain, which is your fee.

It's highly likely there's only one, maybe two objections over the appraised value. After all, how much of a disagreement can there reasonably be? You're either close and you're talking about a difference of a few thousand pounds, or your prospect has unrealistic expectations based on their own naivety or false expectations placed in their minds by your competition. Whatever it is they raise, write those objections down and make sure they've exhausted their thoughts before moving on.

What If There Are No Comparables?

The individuality of the property will dictate what you're able to put forward as a comparable to back up your valuation. Having worked in an area where properties varied hugely, where as a valuer you would see everything from a one-bedroom flat in the morning, to a thatched 'chocolate box' cottage before lunch and a 7-bedroom country farmhouse in the early evening, sometimes it is almost impossible to find direct comparables.

This is where your experience as an estate agent really comes into play. Invariably, you'll be able to bring some comparables to the table such as properties of a similar size or accommodation which have sold in the local area over the last few years and apply some form of calculation based on market value increases. You should also know how sought after the area is.

With highly unique properties, there's an element of letting the market decide what its value is. You have to do your best and it pays to explain to the client how you would normally value the property (based on the above) and tell them how vitally important it is to clear the hurdle of the mortgage valuer also having a say in the value of the home. Inevitably, it will come down to what the client wants for it, tempered against your own 'gut feeling' on whether you feel that's realistic based on the property type, location, and market demand.

Some agents attempt to use square footage/meterage calculations to value properties, and whilst this can give some indications of value, outside of the city centre markets, we do not believe this is any replacement for a true estate agents expert opinion.

As an aside, one of the most frustrating things you can experience as a potential seller is when an agent asks you "what you think it's worth?", before they've provided you with their expert opinion. Quite frankly, even if your prospect does know what it's worth, it's your job to tell them. And by asking this question, agents don't realise how much it sets them up to fail.

Firstly, you're inadvertently asking the client to do your job for you (which is not what you get paid for), and secondly, if the client says some crazy figure backed up by no research whatsoever, you're going to have a hard time convincing them that its unrealistic because you put the ball firmly in their court. The whole reason we go through this delicate journey is to help the client see sense in the proposed marketing price of their property and not put us on the back front at the outset.

Overcoming Price Objections

Once your client has exhausted all their objections in relation to your suggested marketing price, recap what you've written down so you can clarify exactly what they've told you, so you know you've understood it correctly. So, you'd say something like this:

"Mr/s Client, from what you've told me, you're concerned that based on the comparable evidence we have, which the mortgage valuation surveyor is also going to use to value the property on behalf of any buyer, that the price of your property should be higher than what's been suggested. Is that correct?"

Give them an opportunity to confirm what you've just said or to clarify further the point they initially raised Your rephrasing may cause them to rethink their objection.

"Ok great. So, taking that concern into account, can you tell me what evidence you've seen to justify a higher price?"

This question can be a little confronting and is purposely so. Essentially, you're trying to establish if the prospect has seen any evidence from elsewhere that supports a higher price for their property (which you may not be aware of), or whether it is just their personal thoughts and feelings or a genuine misunderstanding. Everyone thinks their property is worth more than their neighbour's home but again, these expectations need to be realistic.

If the difference that you're talking about is a few thousand pounds, you have to make a decision as to whether you want to take on the marketing of the property at the higher figure, with a 'gentleman's agreement' that should it not sell within a few weeks or months, that they will reduce the price to the level you suggested it's worth (and they'll pay you for your marketing costs if it doesn't sell and they withdraw it from sale).

If the client seems to think the property should be advertised at a much higher figure and has little justification for it other than their own personal feelings, press further. To keep rapport at this point, it's worth keeping the conversation light and using some of the objection handling techniques we cover later.

At this stage, you might want to clarify and recap on the points they raised at the start of the appointment concerning why they want to move home. The number one problem with putting a property up for sale at too high a price is that ultimately it won't sell, and it costs you as the agent money and time to try and sell it. This leaves your prospect in a position where they will:

1) Miss out on their dream home when it comes up for sale because they're not ready to go.

2) Will be 'beaten to the punch' by a buyer who has already sold their home or is in a better position to proceed.

3) May not receive any interest from prospective buyers, so they'll get frustrated and will likely become disheartened in an already stressful process. This leaves them on the helter-skelter of price reductions over weeks and months as they attempt to cut the price to attract more interest. This may appear desperate to an opportunist buyer who may low-ball them, leaving them further frustrated or unable to move to the property they really want to buy, or worse, with no option than to accept a low offer to secure the home they want.

4) Peer-pressure from friends and neighbours in the area might also be brought to bear on the client and you don't want them to look foolish if their property is publicly advertised at the higher figure and it fails to sell for months. Peer-pressure can be a very strong motivator for some, causing them to think twice about a rash-decision to advertise at too high a price.

5) There may be objectives they've talked about which you can now re-iterate to your potential client to show how pricing the property too high will likely cause them to fail in meeting their desired outcome(s).

6) As the agent, you'll be wasting hundreds, if not thousands, of pounds on marketing a property that you know you cannot sell at the higher price. You'll also be frustrated and let's be honest, you won't try as hard to sell it as you know its overpriced and the client's

unreasonableness rubs you up the wrong way (obviously you won't be mentioning this point to your client!).

7) Ultimately, even if it does sell at the higher figure and then gets downvalued by a mortgage valuer, your client could cost themselves £2,500+ in abortive legal and other professional fees if their buyer pulls out.

It's important to 'go a couple of rounds' with the prospect to see if they'll see sense. You want to show you've got some tactical negotiation skills now, otherwise just rolling over and going with what the client wants or demands, lets them know you have little skills in this vital area.

And if that's the role you're selling yourself on to your client, you've just proven you're worth about as much as your cut-price competitors…

The objection-handling responses you can use are covered later on so you can hopefully get to a point of agreeing a sensible figure for marketing.

CHAPTER SEVEN

SECRETS TO NEGOTIATING THE SECOND SUMMIT

After you've addressed the client's concerns about price, the next summit of the mountain to scale relates to the fees you want to charge for helping them sell their home, as well as any other additional services you're able to offer. At this point, you're either; calmly walking the client through the presentation with complete agreement on the price and they're broadly happy with you as an agent, or you've hit one or two speedbumps which you've managed to skilfully negotiate, or you're in a position of complete disagreement and you've had to close your folder and walk away from the job.

If you're walking away, the discussion regarding your fees becomes irrelevant. However, assuming you're on the same page at this point, taking the next step to talk about fees is exciting and hopefully a mere formality if you've built good rapport.

Yet for some reason, the fee hurdle is one which paralyses more agents than it should. Agents arrive at their chosen fee by looking at what the competition is doing and copying that, rather than being original with how they provide their service. Fatally, they also largely copy the competition's fee structure.

This places the client in a bit of a bind, and they're left to make a choice between two, three, or more agents without much to distinguish between them. Can you see why the client goes with the lowest fee? They don't know any better so you cannot blame them for making this choice when they've been told by all agents that their home will quickly sell at £X, the service offered is roughly the same, and the fees are the only difference upon which to decide.

Yes, we're repeating this point, but the reason why is because these practices are so ingrained into the industry, it's going to feel uncomfortable when you try to make a change.

The Ultimate Position To Be In

So, the ideal position to be in is to have already done a lot of the value-adding groundwork by nurturing the proposed seller over a decent period of time. If the seller has received say, a quarterly magazine from your agency, full of **useful** information about the local property market and more things of interest to them as a homeowner, do you think this will help keep you at the forefront of their mind and show them that you provide great service?

If the seller has received Christmas cards from your agency over the last few years, is that enough to stick in their minds?

How about when they visited your website and downloaded a 12-page 'Ultimate Guide To Selling Your Home At The Best Possible Price' and not only got an information-packed eBook which can help them achieve the best price for their home (not just a sales pitch for your agency), but they also got enrolled into a nurture program that showed them the best way to prepare for selling their home and what they can do to reduce the timescale and stresses between offer and completion.

From doing the earlier exercise, you'll be able to offer many other helpful bits of information so you can build up several 'touch points' with prospective sellers, so you're already at the forefront of their minds when it comes to selling and your competition doesn't even get a look-in, no matter what level they cut their fee to.

It's worth repeating, agents tend to get distracted with what we call 'ego-driven indicators' where they focus on their market share, or number of boards in an area, or number of properties sold. True, these can be an indicator that your business is doing well, but who would you rather be; the agent with the most boards up in an area (because properties aren't selling at the over-inflated figures they're listed at), or the agent who's making the most profit per property sold and has a stress-free time doing it? There's lots of businesses out there which appear to be doing well on the surface but dive a little deeper into the numbers and they tell a very different story.

Remember, turnover is vanity, profit is sanity.

Investing the time into building your nurture campaign can add significant value to your business and help your potential client to make up their mind that you're the **only** agent to use before they've even thought about putting their property up for sale.

Highlighting The Difference

Making your business another me-too offering isn't going to cut it as we're sure you must realise by now. So, it's essential to draw your strong USP's to your client's attention as you go through your presentation. We've reviewed some of these points already, so make them obvious to your client. Perhaps you've already taken enough photos and details so you can do a quick-mock-up of their sales details on your iPad whilst you're going through the presentation. Telling your client that you can get started immediately, is a powerful position to be in and may just give them the nudge they need to pull the trigger.

Maybe you use professional photography or drone footage in your marketing so you can show them the difference it makes through a visual presentation right there in front of your client. This is especially powerful if you can use a property that was on the market with one of your competitors that you then sold. You can show them the difference between static photos (especially if they're poor-quality photos the agent used), and your bright, professional photos with drone footage which gives people an expert walk-through of their home.

Perhaps you can show how you saved a client £10,000, £20,000 or more on the purchase of their new home, just by stepping in and handling all the negotiations on their behalf? This can be incredibly powerful for clients who are not expert negotiators and who hate the prospect of having to bargain for their new home or face rejection, so reluctantly pay the asking price (which is most people).

As a quick example, some years ago, we surveyed a property on behalf of some friends. It was clear there was a great deal more work to be done on it than they realised (for example, the plaster had begun to de-bond from the brick walls). We suggested they start substantially below the asking price with their first offer, which to their credit they did. When the agent refused however, their second offer was the full asking price…

(Incidentally, this was the only house we've ever gone round where the coffee table exhibited a large tub of Vaseline and a large box of tissues (with used ones by the side) **does mini-sick in mouth**)

Maybe you can show how you managed to find another client their dream home that wasn't even on the market, simply because you're well connected and that's what you do. Or how you helped a landlord client secure some great deals on investment properties which made them a healthy profit or great return.

Whatever it is, you have a wealth of experience, so you must highlight this to your client. They don't know what you know, or what you've been through to get your knowledge and experience, so show them!

Incidentally, if you're reading this and saying to yourself, "that's fine for you to say Silas, but I don't have this knowledge and experience in these areas!" then you simply need to start doing things differently than how you've always done them.

Experiment with your service offering. Try new things. See if you can flush out the ideal home for your potential clients and matchmake the two. What's the worst that can happen?

Your agency is not a Dr Pepper advert! Make some mistakes! After all, that's one of the ways you'll learn, and you never know, you might stumble onto something amazing which becomes your 'secret sauce' in your service offering.

(And in case you don't know, some of the biggest discoveries which have led to companies taking off were made entirely by accident, so there's something to be said about conducting an experiment with your service offering to see what works and what doesn't).

Winning BIG Fees

Being able to introduce your client to an alternative fee structure which stacks the odds in both your favours works well if you're hitting resistance from them to pay a flat fee. Here, we mean demonstrating how you can, using your awesome negotiation skills, save them thousands, if not tens of thousands, of pounds off the purchase price of their next home. And in doing so, you charge them for your professional assistance.

Remember, most people hate negotiating and if you're offering to take this nerve-racking process away from them, they will thank you for it. It's a very easy way to help yourself earn an extra half a percentage point (or more) on the purchase price of the home they're thinking of buying. Or structure the deal based on paying you £100 per £1,000 in savings you make on the purchase price; they get the benefit of 90% for each £1,000 you save them. That's got to be a win-win.

There are many ways you can structure these types of deals when you start to get creative. A 2% fee on the sale of their home may be too much to bear. But throw in the fact that you'll negotiate the purchase of the one they're buying on their behalf, and suddenly 2% becomes cheap!

Also, think about whether you can offer a sliding scale for your fees based on reducing your fees if you don't sell their home within a certain timeframe. Let's say they'll pay you 2% for a sale within 12 weeks, 1.5% between 12-26 weeks and 1% thereafter, incentivising you to sell their property quickly.

Different Levels Of Service

As you've already gone through the intense process of identifying all the potential problems your clients may face in moving home journey, you should have an exhaustive list, along with all the possible solutions you could offer them to solve all of these headaches, and the vehicles you can employ to deliver these services.

This is a very exciting place to be as you can now start looking at how you use these many solutions to offer different levels of packaged services to your target audience.

But before you do, perhaps time to have a quick stretch and a cup of tea!

Ok, back to it!

One of the main frustration's agents face (which is of their own making), is going into a negotiation with a potential client, to win an instruction on a 'take-it-or-leave-it' basis.

As we saw earlier, most agents put forward a price they think they can achieve for the home and then suggest a fee they'll charge the owner for selling it. What this does, (which is bad for agents), is place the client in the uncomfortable and confrontational situation of saying yes or no to that offer. As such, agents are put in a position where they'll lose more than they win.

Better thinking would be to remove the yes or no element and offer different options to your prospect, such as Gold, Silver, and Bronze packages. It's rare to see professional services packaged up in this way, however, think about how different the selling experience would be received by your prospective client. Offering three different levels of service switches the conversation from the 'take-it-or-leave-it' scenario, to one where you outline each one, then ask them which they prefer.

By doing so, it's easier to show your prospect the difference in value between the packages and prices you're charging for each one. Think about it from their point of view, it's unlikely any other agent will be offering them the solutions to their problems, packaged in a way that is affordable and takes away all the stress, worry, and frustration.

For example, let's look at what might be the differences between your Gold, Silver, and Bronze packages. Starting with the Bronze package, you might decide to offer a no-frills service to the client. You offer to help them sell their property via all the usual marketing methods and you'll charge them 1.25% for doing so, with the same service offering that's commoditised and likely in alignment with the rest of your competition.

In your Silver package, you might decide to offer accompanied viewings and help the client by negotiating the purchase of the property they want to buy. For this, you might charge them 1.75%.

At the Gold level, you decide to offer your highest level of service, such as personally viewing every property your clients are thinking about buying and providing your expert opinion on what you feel the property is worth, whether it's in a good area or not, and whether the property will be worth spending the sort of money on that they're thinking of investing. You might also organise introductions to your elite level team members who can help them put the deal together and buy it in the shortest possible timeframe. You might also offer out of hours viewings and give them access to your complete library of training videos and PDF's. At this level, you could be charging 2+%, but the important point is, the client can see the difference in value between the packages and now has a yardstick with which to evaluate each package against your competition. But your competition won't be offering the same. And that's a powerful position to be in because it puts you in a category of one.

And if you're wondering if this could really work for you, something which is mostly overlooked in marketing, is that people like to buy expensive things, they just need an excuse to do so. Remember, there are people who will spend more money on a handbag than you're charging for all the countless hours of blood, sweat, and tears you're going to invest in helping them sell their property! So don't ever doubt the fact that they'll buy, especially if you package it in the right way, and present it in a way that makes it almost illogical to say no to.

After all, that's your skill as an agent, right..? Negotiating…?

Because your competition is unlikely to present their services in this way, and they'll merely verbally run through their pre-prepared script of what they'll do for their fee, your competitive advantage becomes helping the client pick from the menu, the service level that's right for them. You're not offering the usual 'one size fits all' approach. Thus, your customers feel they're choosing something a little more 'tailor-made' for their needs and indeed, you may even decide this is the right way to offer your exclusive services to the market. This positioning also may leave the client with the feeling that what your competition are offering is in some way inferior, even though you're not saying it (and you never should say it in our professional opinion). Merely offer what you offer and let the power of your marketing do the rest.

And by the way, have you ever noticed when three options are presented to prospects, one is usually labelled 'best value' whilst another is labelled 'most popular'? Just food for thought when you're running through these options with your clients…

If you want to know how you can really add value to your clients and your business, there's a ton of extra resources we can share with you on a call.

We just ask you to invest 30 minutes into a complimentary consultation, where we can help fast-track your success (with no hard sell whatsoever).

Here's the link to book your call:

http://www.wiggywam.co.uk/estateagentssecretscall

CHAPTER EIGHT

THE SECRET POWER OF
SCARCITY AND URGENCY

Something we've seen zero agents do, is operate in a way which creates scarcity and urgency in the marketplace to generate increased client demand for their services.

Agents are usually so keen to please, they make themselves available 24 hours a day, seven days a week and they literally cannot do enough to help and support a client. Whilst this is admirable, it commoditises your business because there's no urgent reason for a client to work with you. They can take their time to decide who they want to work with.

As an analogy, why is a car such as a Ferrari, Bugatti, or Lamborghini <u>so</u> much more expensive than say a Ford, Vauxhall, or Rover? Aside from the differences in specifications, there's a huge rarity factor which causes high demand from people who want to buy a sports car which is in very limited supply, versus a much higher supply of lower cost cars which are functional but lack the performance of a prestige marque. Could Ferrari, Bugatti, and Lamborghini reduce their prices and pump out more vehicles to meet the high demand? Probably, but then they would lose the element of scarcity and demand would likely fall as a result.

Remember, most people want something they cannot have.

Think about your sales process from a slightly different perspective. If you were literally inundated with clients who all wanted to work with you, were at full capacity and couldn't take another client on for at least a few weeks, how much would this help to frame things in your client's mind? You're showing social proof that there's high demand to work with you, and not only that, but people are also prepared to pay higher fees for the higher levels of service you obviously provide.

How would your prospect likely act if you were to offer not only the Gold, Silver, and Bronze packages, but you told the client you only have capacity to offer one more space to work with you on the Gold package this month? For any client who's serious about selling their property and who wants to work with you at the highest level of service you provide, they're more likely to say yes if there's only one space left and they want it, rather than dillydallying about whether to instruct you or if they might get a better deal elsewhere.

Remember FOMO from earlier?

Yup, they suddenly got a bad case of Fear Of Missing Out!

The reason you want to create scarcity and FOMO is because it focusses the prospects mind to realise there's only one of you and only you are offering this elite level of service. This rarity naturally creates scarcity, and an urgent situation where the client must make a decision now or lose the opportunity forever. Whilst this might seem like sales tactics, what you're effectively doing is selectively offering your client a high-level service with the personal touch, at much higher value, so they can make the most out of the opportunity of working with you. A higher fee means you can dedicate more personal one-on-one time with your client.

It's no service at all to your clients, to traumatise yourself and your business by selling your services so cheaply, you cannot afford to dedicate the time, energy, and effort necessary to give them the personal attention and one-on-one service they want (but perhaps didn't verbalise) ...

Not only could you offer one Gold place and two Silver spots, but also offer upgrade opportunities to your clients once they're on board. This effectively means they start with the Bronze or Silver level of service, but if they're not getting the results they want or change their minds later, you can always offer them the potential to upgrade to the higher service level (and price point) of the Silver or Gold package.

This is polar opposite to what most agents do, which is agreeing to reduce their fees along the way, especially as they get closer to exchange of contracts and want the deal to happen or after the 12-week marketing agreement has expired. It flips the script completely, from selling from a place of 'desperation' to selling from an empowered place as the expert in your field, and if the client doesn't act, the opportunity will be lost forever.

A Word Of Warning

There's something which we would hope doesn't need to be said to professional agents like you, but based on experience, it's worth mentioning here. A lot of agents make the mistake of referring to the competition in a very negative way in front of their prospective clients. They mistakenly believe that if they tell the client how bad the competition is, the client will think twice about using them. The fact is, such agents are kicking themselves in the pants, by coming across as highly unprofessional to their potential client.

Don't bad-mouth your competition.

EVER.

It's that simple.

And to be honest, there's no need to. You're a property professional, so don't stoop to the lows of your competitors. Your client won't thank you for it. In fact, we've lost track of the number of sellers who chose us as their agent, simply because a competitor had tried to bad-mouth us.

However, using examples of situations where you have <u>outperformed</u> your competitors can be extremely powerful. Showing potential clients a property which was previously on the market with one of your competitors, and spelling out what you achieved for them once they switched over to you really helps to tip the balance in your favour. Showing two or three examples is even better.

Just don't rubbish your competition. Simply stick to the facts, rather than your opinion.

Putting Your Worst Foot Forward

Let's be frank; your clients expect you to put your best foot forward and tell them you're capable of delivering the impossible when it comes to acting for them to sell their home. The problem is, every agent is saying the same thing, so your client is naturally going to be at least a little bit sceptical about what you say.

Something which virtually no agent uses is 'showing weakness' to their clients, to the point of even admitting their faults. When you admit imperfections, you're going to stand out head and shoulders above the rest. It doesn't have to be revealing your very worst points but making a small admission of your weaknesses can win you huge brownie points as far as your clients are concerned.

Think about it from a dating point of view. When you go on a first date with someone, you're both likely to be talking a great game about who you are and what you have to offer. That's expected. But when you make small, vulnerable admissions of imperfections, this can really make anyone genuine be drawn to you. And if it puts them off, then they weren't the right partner for you anyway. It works the same way with clients.

So, think about what admissions you could make to prospects that will help you be seen as more vulnerable and believable. Perhaps you're incredibly busy with deals right now and you must admit that you don't always get back to clients before the 5:30pm going home time. But you do make up for this by emailing clients with an update at 10pm, just to maintain the high levels of service your clients have come to expect from you.

Or perhaps your admission is that your passion for the job sometimes affects your family life because you've been known to take a diversion whilst driving your family to a weekend away by doing a viewing of a property that was 'en-route'.

What about how you frequently forget things at the supermarket because clients old and new stop you and ask for advice whilst you're doing the weekly shop? Whilst this sometimes makes your partner mad, you can't help but share your expertise freely with those who ask.

Or how you failed to sell the last three homes that went on the market at a price higher than what you valued them at? But they were sold several months later after the clients reduced them to the figures you'd originally appraised them at.

Whatever it is, it <u>must be true</u> and not put you in too bad a light with your clients. Just enough to admit you're human like everybody else and you're capable of making mistakes. You'll be amazed at how this can draw your clients to you like moths to a flame.

The admission of an imperfection in you and/or your service will skyrocket your credibility and make you more believable, simply because they'll feel if you're willing to admit an imperfection, you must be being <u>totally</u> honest with them about everything else you say. So, make sure you are!

Overcome Objections Like An Olympic Hurdler

We've covered a lot of ground so far, so we hope you've found it useful and its given you inspiration. Let's get right into how to nail client objections which come up as you move towards asking your client for their business.

At this stage of the appointment, you should have done a good enough job at building rapport if you've correctly identified their personality type and done a good job at mixing and matching. So, keep in mind the amount of work you've done. By now, you've hopefully positioned yourself as the prospect's trusted advisor (and perhaps even their friend).

Yet the biggest stumbling block comes towards the end of the presentation when it's time to ask for the business and close the deal. The overwhelming number of agents fear rejection so play it safe by saying something like, "we'll write to you", as they scurry out the door! If you're one of these people, we want to share a secret which we guarantee your competition won't know and it's this; there's very little difference between the emotions of excitement and nervousness. In fact, if you ponder this and think about how your body reacts with these two emotions, you'll see that they're actually very similar.

So, when you're about to ask for the business, and your palms are sweaty, knees weak, arms are heavy, on the surface you look calm and ready, to drop bombs…(sorry, we couldn't resist ha ha) you feel your heart race and your breathing becomes shallower, tell yourself you're excited and watch what a difference it makes. You'll be amazed. It's a lot easier to create the outcome you want from a place of excitement and joy, rather than being fearful of rejection.

And when you're excited about asking for the business, rather than carrying a fear of rejection, you'll be miles ahead of all your competition who are too afraid to even ask in the first place.

But in our experience, asking once for the business is just not enough.

Studies have shown that prospects will usually say 'no' up to eight times, before they will say 'yes'. So, knowing most people will likely say yes if you ask ten times, then you've just discovered the number one secret to winning business.

But as in dating and in life, no-one likes a stalker or a weirdo, so you have to do this with panache, decorum, and with a smile on your face that knows no defeat!

Think about sitting opposite someone on a first date and they say to you, "Will you marry me?" How's that going to go down? Beyond the truly desperate, or the one in a million meeting of true soulmates, most will run a mile. The main reason being, they've not taken the time to really get to know one another and more importantly, to demonstrate the value they can bring to the table.

It's very similar with your pitch for business – make sure you've shown incredible value to your client as we've been talking about throughout this book, so when you ask for their business, they're ready to hand it to you on a silver platter.

Features -v- Benefits

Just as a quick aside, one of the biggest mistakes salespeople make when pitching their client, is they talk about <u>features</u> of their product or service. Yet, the client doesn't care about those features; **only what benefits they**

get from them. So, think about this carefully when it comes to positioning your service with your client.

No-one cares about side-impact bars on cars. But tell someone this revolutionary system has been proven to save peoples lived in the event of an accident and suddenly, your client is motivated. One's a feature. The other is a huge <u>benefit</u>.

So, don't tell them you put all your properties on the internet (feature), tell them all your properties go on a magical, 24/7, international sales platform which drives enquiries from every corner of the globe where eager buyers are keen to find a property like theirs; the benefit is that it will help them sell their home far more quickly, and for a better price when combined with your expertise.

Don't tell them you offer accompanied viewings (feature), tell them that your accompanied viewing service is highly recommended to those clients who want their agent to work their butts off for their commission by putting their time, energy, and expertise into doing the viewings for them, so the buyers can feel totally at ease dealing with an independent person who can answer all of their questions; the ultimate benefit being, they don't have to stress about what to say, or risk being put in a corner when someone tries to negotiate the price of their home directly.

Finally, you might notice the difference between stating a feature of your service, and the passion which comes across from describing why you offer something and what the ultimate benefits are to your client for doing so. When you do this verbally, its salesmanship. Copywriting is salesmanship in print, and the benefits this can bring to your business are enormous when you get it right.

In effect, by using copywriting in all your marketing materials, you're creating an army of virtual salespeople who go out and bring you business, but in a way which means the client convinces themselves you're the right person for the job based on the journey you've taken them on in their minds eye from the powerful copy you've written.

In short, the words you use should conjure up visual images in people's minds causing them to experience feelings which they associate with consuming your content. And when you do this to the point of creating tension within your prospect, they'll more than likely act on your 'call to action' to relieve this tension.

Its powerful, so make some time to study copywriting if you want to amplify your results.

CHAPTER NINE

SECRETS TO TURBO-BOOST YOUR RESULTS

If you want to add mad value to your clients, use this massive secret: offer bonuses to help close the deal and win the instruction.

What do we mean when we suggest offering bonuses? Well, let's revisit the list of problems and solutions you pulled together earlier. Once you've compiled all the possible different solutions, you can offer these as potential 'signing-on' bonuses to the client, for taking action and making a decision to work with you today.

In practice, you've created several different resources, and depending upon which of the three packages a client chooses, you could offer two different bonuses which are only available if they sign up now. Not only does this further increase the perceived value you're offering your clients, there's implied scarcity, which suggests if they don't sign up soon, they will lose out forever.

The reason this is so powerful is because it creates a price-to-value discrepancy, which caused the buyer tension, and a sense of urgency to buy now. Remember the hidden secret of perceived value from earlier? Now you'll see why we've gone on about it so much…

For example, let's say you decide to offer a particular value-add solution to your client as a bonus, provided they sign up now. This should ideally be low-cost to you, but of high value to your client. If you took all of your negotiating skills and expertise and put it into a guide. This guide might be <u>worth</u> something like, £1,000 to your client.

Why?

Because by using your negotiating tactics, they may be able to knock £10-20,000+ off the property they want to buy. Or better still, use your negotiating techniques for the rest of their lives on <u>everything</u> they buy…

This has significant <u>value</u> to your clients, but by providing this guide in PDF or eBook format, <u>costs</u> you virtually nothing to produce. What you're doing is price-anchoring the value of £1,000 in your client's mind, which, when compared to the overall <u>price</u> of your service package, starts to make the overall <u>value</u> look incredible.

Dan Kennedy, a famous marketing guru, suggests the secret to sales is to make offers to prospects which are so good, they feel stupid saying no!

Applying this thinking to your business and giving away bonuses to help people which have values of £1,000, £2,000 or more, upsets the price-to-value ratio in the client's mind as they start to think that paying your fees just to get these incredible bonuses makes everything an absolute bargain (and they'd be stupid if they said no!).

Think of offering them £50 notes for just £5 – that's enough to make anyone walk over broken glass to grab the opportunity you're waving under their nose! No longer are they just paying you a certain percentage to sell their home; they're getting incredibly valuable information which can save them (tens of), thousands.

Here's the hidden secret which no-one will tell you. If you get this right, the value of your bonuses alone begins to dwarf the actual cost of your commission. You might want to re-read that last sentence a few times until the penny drops…

The other alternative is for the client to say no to working with you, and in doing so, they're turning down your expertise and the incredibly valuable bonuses you're offering.

Now, some agents might ask; "If people know all of my secrets by consuming all my training materials, won't they simply decide to buy, sell, or rent their property themselves and not use me?"

This might seem like a rational question, but if you look at your own life and how busy you are, how many people have realistically got the time, effort,

ESTATE AGENT'S SECRETS – VOLUME II - ENGAGE

knowledge, and expertise to do all this themselves, when they haven't moved home in 5-10 years, (and in truth, lack the ability to negotiate a sensible purchase for their next property)? The answer is precious few.

So, most people will choose to 'pay away the pain' by employing you to do the heavy lifting for them rather than trying to do it all themselves to save a few quid (and running the painful risk of failing). Think about the bathroom example where someone trying to do it themselves risks messing it up and having their wife screaming at them versus paying someone else to do it and transferring the blame to them if something goes wrong.

Hopefully, you can see the benefits of combining a number of these secret strategies together, and in doing so, putting yourself into your very own Blue Ocean.

Perception Is Reality

We've mentioned Perception Is Reality a lot in this book as it's such an important concept for agents reading this to understand. The secret is, it's vitally important because perception is what drives most human psychology, and ultimately most buying decisions.

Think about this example for a minute.

Why would anyone pay £1,000, £10,000 or even £11,000,000 (the most expensive ever sold), for a handbag when it's possible to buy one from the local market for less than £20? Apart from the slightly obvious answer about the quality, the main reason why people pay such inflated amounts, is because a perception of value is created through the exclusivity of the expensive handbag and how others will perceive its owner, knowing there might only be one or two of them available in the whole world.

When certain fashion items are promoted in such a way to make people appreciate a handbag costs £10,000, the public's perception is that someone who carries a £10,000 handbag must be very wealthy. Even if they spent so much on the bag itself, they have very little money inside it, the perception is the owner has money, wealth, and status. And if you know anything about marketing, these are powerful motivations which cause people to buy…

Why is it important for us to understand the concept of perception in our business? Because so many are trying to create a perception of success. There are tons of people who choose to lease a car rather than own one, simply because the monthly payments on the lease hire agreements are less than it would cost them to own the car outright as a cash purchase, or to buy the car on finance and have the hassle of running costs and servicing.

Lease agreements also offer a way for people to drive a more expensive car than they might otherwise be able to. The secret reason is, anybody who does this is because they want to give the perception that they're successful. This spills into all areas of a person's life including the money they spend on makeup, the clothes they wear, the house they live in, and which restaurants they choose to eat at.

The main point to realise is, we're all guilty of making judgements about others, based on their outer appearances, and despite the problems judging a book by its cover can cause, we're all guilty of it to one extent or another. When we see someone driving up to view a million-pound home in an old clunker of a car, chances are we automatically dismiss them as being unable to afford it. Even though many of the seriously wealthy will look like they've not got two pennies to rub together and are happy flying under the radar of public perception…

So, here's the big secret to lock into your business and marketing: all people love receiving value for money, and no-one likes to be ripped off. So, if you're the one who offers the perception of value for money with your products and services, where the client *perceives* they're receiving far more value in exchange for the money they're spending, you're going to move quickly away from the rest of the pack (even if your competition is charging less).

One of the nuances of perception is reality is, the more expensive something is, the more desirable it tends to become in the eyes of the consumer. Think about buying a watch versus buying a Rolex – which one conjures up feelings of desire to own it, despite being 10-100 times more expensive than a run of the mill model?

It's vitally important for us to get our heads round this concept, because as an agent, you have an opportunity to increase the desirability of your more expensive service packages, providing there's more perceived value than the client is giving up in cash value.

Perceived Value

The idea of perceived value is even more important when it comes to pricing your services in the marketplace. As we saw earlier, it's possible to offer value which is wildly different from the actual cost a customer or client pays.

For example, if you go to a bookshop and pick up a non-fiction book priced at £20, the value is incredible because of the knowledge that can be gained from spending a few hours reading. Usually, an author has put a lifetime of experiences into the pages of the book yet is providing access to their knowledge for a fraction of the cost a professional consultation with them would cost. Despite the small cost of the book, the <u>application</u> of the knowledge you gain could be worth thousands of pounds to you (Hint: the same applies with <u>this</u> book and the other two volumes!).

Taking this a step further, if you liked what the author said, you might then decide to invest more money into their other programs such as coaching or mentoring to help you get the results you want. So, you check out the authors website and decide to invest £97 in an audio program or invest £200 in their eBook and audiobook package. Or you might go all in and stump up £497 for a video training course to explore further some of the topics discussed in the book in greater detail. Finally, you might extend this to £2,000 to attend a three-day seminar by the author which adds massive value to your business by helping you to implement exactly what you've learnt.

The point is there's different levels of value being offered at different price points.

You can use this to your advantage in your own business. As we touched on in the client nurturing process, we can distil some of our knowledge and wisdom into a PDF or eBook that if we were to sell on its own to a cold audience, we might be lucky to get £9.97 for or maybe even £19.97 with a lot of time invested in selling.

However, the value you're providing is substantially higher, so a client's perception might be the value of that PDF or eBook could be as high as

£497. Do you see the difference? As a stand-alone item for sale, it could be a low-ticket item, but bundled into a package of other products and services or offered as a bonus, its value can be significantly more.

(If it seems like we're repeating ourselves, it's because this is so important to drill down on because it's the secret to transforming your business. So, stick with it until you've fully grasped what we're saying, and you're taking action to implement it).

Hopefully by now, you can see that adding such information products, a video training series or in-person service, either as a bonus, or as part of a packaged service offer, you're creating a significant price to value discrepancy which will compel your prospect to act and grab themselves a great deal or lose out.

Let's work through an example, so you can see exactly how this works in practice.

Let's say you normally sell a £100,000 property for a flat fee of 1% plus VAT. In cash value, the fee you'll earn is simply £1,000, assuming you don't charge extra for marketing expenses etc. and £200 going to the tax man.

In the client's mind, the minimum they must spend is £1,000 plus VAT (£1,200), to achieve their desired end result, which is to sell their property for £100,000.

Now, let's go one step further and suggest out of three agents (including you), two agents are charging 1% and have both valued the property at the same price. You come in as the third agent and even if you've decided to ignore everything in these books about increasing fees and are still prepared to do the sale at 1%, you also offer the client several other valuable resources to help them out.

Say you offered three additional bonuses to your service, which rather than bundle them up into one package and slap a price on it, you simply decide to break them down into separate units to explain their individual value to your prospect.

First, you created 'The Ultimate Guide To Buying Your Next Home At Half The Price' which is a 15-page eBook showing all the different skills they could use to find a property and negotiate on it like their life depended on it. You could easily state the value of this eBook is at least £297.

Second, you offer your prospect access to your VIP video training suite, which is an exclusive offer for them to gain an insane amount of knowledge which they can't get anywhere else (even from your competition). You describe this value add as being worth at least £597.

Third, you offer them a quick signing-on bonus, for today only, of your guide called, 'Building Your Power Team Effortlessly & Easily So You Can Remove The Frustration Most Experience When Moving Home', which shows them how one wrong team member can cost them dearly through lost sleep, tons of stress, worry, and frustration. This, you assure your prospect, is worth at least £197, and is only available for those clients who sign up with you today.

Who wouldn't want access to this sort of information…? And if they didn't get it, not only are they grossly unprepared when entering the property market, they'll be going up against people who do have it, and so they'll likely lose out on the best deal on their next home and experience all the stress and frustration you're trying to help them avoid with all your expert knowledge.

Now, the secret psychological trick is, the additional information products start to build huge value in the client's mind. Not only are they getting the eBook for £297, but they're also getting the VIP training video suite valued at £597, and another eBook worth £197. Suddenly, assuming they sign with you today, they're getting nearly £1,100 worth of additional bonus value for the same £1,000 they would have to pay your competition anyway.

A more interesting psychological secret is the fact that humans will likely take more action to horde a perceived precious resource, (even if they don't use it), rather than missing out. So, the client is faced with paying £1,000 to you to receive £2,100 worth of value or paying £1,000 to your competition AND LOSING £1,100 worth of precious resources that could really help them. Plus, how are they going to feel when faced with three options, but they turn down the one which offers the most value? Pretty f*cking stupid!

When you look at it like this, who would you rather place your business with? It's a complete no-brainer, isn't it? By offering this extra value, you would have to do something silly to lose the job when you're offering such a valuable package on the battlefield of mediocre competition.

But does this only work with the lower end of the market, you ask? Well, let's explore that shall we?

Suppose you're selling properties in the £1,000,000+ price bracket and the fees are still 1% plus VAT. That's a tasty £10,000 fee assuming you can sell the property. And if it's a desirable and fast-selling area, some agents might cut their fee to the bone and charge less than 1% to hit their monthly targets.

Would offering the three bonuses we talked about earlier worth £1,000 really make that much of a difference to a client when they're deciding who to go with? The short answer is yes. Apart from the seller finding the documents well written (assuming they are), they demonstrate a pro-active approach by the agent, and combined with the client nurturing journey you'll put them through, you begin to stand out even more.

At this level, you could also offer a more personal 'concierge' service by offering to negotiate the purchase of their new home could almost certainly save them £10,000 or more. So, the value of your bonuses merely escalates in proportion to the value of the properties you're selling and the value of the packages you wish to offer. Make sense?

This makes the overall price you're charging pale into insignificance against the value the client receives. And even if you're operating in the ultra-high price bracket properties of £10,000,000+ the scope to offer higher perceived value services increases exponentially because you can afford to spend more on service delivery than those agents working at the other end of the market.

By now, you can see the sense in not only creating these resources, but actually using them as bonuses or as additional products to boost the value of your overall service offering, allowing you to comfortably win more instructions and increase your fees with little client resistance. After all, the only reason why a client will argue the fee with you is either because they're Indian (said lovingly being married into an Indian family!), or because they don't see the value in what you're offering. And when two or more service providers offer the same service for the same price, surely one will accept less if they really want the business?

Do yourself and your business a favour by investing some time into designing a new level of service, which requires you to spend a little time building out some evergreen information products to put yourself into your very own Blue Ocean Strategy where you're not worried about your throat being cut in a race to the bottom by your competitors.

The Ultimate Authority Builder

On final reflection, we decided to bump The Ultimate Authority Builder secret into Volume III and when you read it, you'll understand why. This secret strategy is ultra-powerful, but without the solid foundation in your business, it'll stick out like a sore thumb and won't give you the true benefits it otherwise would.

You can grab a copy of Estate Agent's Secret's Volume III here: http://www.wiggywam.co.uk/estateagentssecretstrilogy

If you want to know how you can really add value to your clients and your business, there's a ton of extra resources we can share with you on a call.

We just ask you to invest 30 minutes into a complimentary consultation, where we can help fast-track your success (with no hard sell whatsoever).

Here's the link to book your call:

http://www.wiggywam.co.uk/estateagentssecretscall

CHAPTER TEN

THE SECRETS TO OVERCOMING OBJECTIONS

For anyone who has seen the movie Boiler Room, you'll know what a rebuttal is. For everyone else, a rebuttal can essentially be described as an automatic comeback you make to your client that not only overcomes their objection but puts you in a position where you can ask for the business again. When you watch someone who must make lots of cold calls every day to make a living, they very quickly map out a way to build rapport quickly with the prospect to help break their routine, strike up conversation, find common ground, win them over, and then ask for their business, sometimes in the space of only a few minutes.

We're not suggesting you operate as a 'Boiler Room', but what's worth doing is working hard on your rebuttals. When you ask for the business and move the client towards agreeing to work with you and sign on the dotted line, you'll quickly find there will be several common objections which come up repeatedly. Sure, they won't be worded the exact same way by every client, but the essence of the objections will be the same. And once you know this, you'll have your trusted responses on standby to use at exactly the right moment so you can continually win trust and get your client to agree to do business with you.

It's worth writing down all the common client objections from lots number of different appointments (which you'll do anyway as you put this book into practice), so you can recognise the common patterns as they emerge. Then, you want to craft your rebuttals in such a way that they cover the following points:

1) It must not make the client feel wrong or make them look foolish.
2) It ought to reassure the client and demonstrate value.

3) It must be true & honest.
4) It ought to position you as their trusted advisor and friend.
5) It ought to automatically lead you to ask for the business again.

What you'll likely find is that you'll eventually run a circular pattern that goes something like this:

a) You ask for their business
b) They make an objection (or essentially an excuse)
c) You handle their objection with a rebuttal which ends in asking for their business again
d) They make an objection (or essentially an excuse)
e) You handle their objection with a rebuttal which ends in asking for their business again
f) And so the cycle continues until you've overcome all their objections, they agree to work with you, or they throw you out the door!

The secret to doing this well is to do it with a smile and a relaxed manner whilst also having built up a ton of value beforehand. Because if what you're offering doesn't excite the prospect, there's no way a rebuttal cycle will work as there's not enough desire from the client in the first place, so you'll just end up pissing them off.

Common Objections

Let's take a look at some of the common objections from clients that come up when you ask for the business and also look at how we can respond with a rebuttal that meets all the criteria above.

Objection #1:

"I'm not one to make decisions quickly! I need to think it over!"

"I don't like being asked to make decisions quickly!"

"I don't like being sold to!"

"I'm committed to using you, I just need to go away and do XXX and then come back to you."

"I need to consult with my partner before we can commit."

"I want to go away and think about it."

"I never commit on the day"

Rebuttal:

"That's fine Mr/s Client. Obviously, you wouldn't take your time thinking this over if you weren't seriously interested, would you? So, may I assume you will give this decision very careful consideration? (They'll obviously say yes!). Just to clarify my thinking, what part of this is it that you need to think over? Is there something we've forgotten to cover? Seriously, please level with me, could it be the investment in our professional services we're asking you to make?"

OR

"Obviously you have a reason for saying that. Would you mind sharing it with me?"

OR

"May I ask you, what exactly do you need to think over?"

If they refuse to give you an answer, or give you what you feel is a watered-down version of the truth, you can follow up with:

"How can I help you with your thinking process? What areas in particular do you need to think through?"

OR

"What questions do you have that, if answered, would really help you in your decision-making process?"

"And is it fair to say, that if we can answer those questions to your satisfaction, then you'll be able to make a decision?" (They should say yes unless they're fobbing you off).

"So, please feel free to ask me anything and I will do my best to help you find the answers you're looking for so that you can make the right decision."

The client will likely give you some thoughts which you should write down in front of them, so you can address them when the time is right to do so. This works best when you are seen to be writing the questions or concerns down, and taking a keen interest, without interrupting them, before saying something along the lines of:

"Ok, so [quick recap of their concern], is there anything else that's bothering you?"

The key here is to make sure you have all the client's objections, questions, or concerns in front of you, so they're all there on paper to be addressed. This does three things:

1. Concerns on paper aren't nearly as frightening as they may appear in your client's mind (don't forget, they're constantly nervous about getting screwed!).

2. By listing their concerns, taking a keen interest, and not interrupting them, your prospective client will feel 'heard'; a crucial part in building rapport and showing you have a genuine interest in their concerns and not just in winning the business.

3. Your client probably feels they have a bigger number of concerns than they actually do, which is very common when we try to manage a lot of thoughts in our head at the same time. Did you know, the brain counts one, two, three, many, as it cannot juggle three or more competing thoughts at any one time without becoming overwhelmed? By listing all objections out on paper and recapping them, you'll find your client rarely gets past five concerns which can then be easily addressed in turn.

Once you have your client's concerns in front of you and they've run out of steam, you then have the advantage of going back and answering each concern in order. It's worth saying something like this;

"So, just to be clear, assuming we can find answers to these questions or concerns I have in front of me, is there anything else that's likely to prevent you from making a decision today?"

Then shut up.

The client will either say no, or list some more concerns that need to be added to your list. This second group of objections may not actually be related to the first and may in fact be your client reacting to feeling like they're in a pressure-cooker environment and are throwing objection after objection at you in the hope that you'll just leave them alone. Monitor how they're feeling and if you think you're pushing too hard, take a few moments before pushing back gently with your rebuttals.

When you're certain your client has given you all their objections, go through each point you've written down, do a quick recap of the issue concerned, address it in a way that gives them maximum benefits, and once you've finished, be seen to put a big tick through the concern to show it's been dealt with, and the client's mind should now be at peace.

A quick secret share: when you're handling client concerns, you want to do so in a way that gives them maximum perceived benefits. So, let's say their concern revolves around you not being the agent that can get them the best price for their home. You would want to address it along the lines of the following:

"So, I understand you have a concern about whether we are the best agent to get you the best possible price for your home – is that correct? (Wait for them to acknowledge you've understood their concerns correctly). Well, first of all, thank you for raising this concern with me as I appreciate it takes a lot to do so. So, what I would like to do is to show you some examples of properties we've sold recently where we were able to achieve more than the asking price."

Then walk them through examples where you have sold properties (ideally like theirs which you will have prepared before the appointment), either by private treaty, online, or physical auction examples, or sealed bids etc. where you can show you sold them in excess of the asking price. Or better still, where your competition valued the property at less than you did, and you achieved the higher price!

Then press your client to see if you've answered their concerns correctly and if they now feel more reassured. Assuming they say yes, then thank them and ask them for their business again by saying something like; "Thank you, that's great to know. Shall we go ahead and put the property on the market?"

Objection #2:

"Your fee is a lot of money. I could save that by doing it myself or using a free agent like Strike!"

"Your fee is more than (twice) that of your competition. Why should I pay you extra?"

Rebuttal:

"Can I ask you a quick question?" Wait for them to say yes.

"Are you really serious about selling or do you only have a casual interest?" Invariably they will suggest they're serious, so follow up with;

"And just suppose you are serious; do you honestly feel you can do this without our expert help to get you the best price for your property? (Don't wait for a response). I must be honest with you and say in my experience, those who have tried to do this on their own have made sizeable mistakes which cost them a lot of money. Let me ask you this, are you financially able to make a mistake which costs you £20,000 or more?

If their response is a highly unlikely 'yes', then ask them if they really want to? More often however, they won't be in a position to say this, so ask them;

"Why do you want to take that risk? Our job is to protect your interests by getting you the best price for your home. That way, we more than pay for ourselves through the service we provide. I'm sure you've got more than enough to worry about with your day-to-day life, and I can assure you that our most successful clients play to their strengths and let us shoulder the burden of selling their home for the best price whilst they get on with their lives, knowing they have made a sound decision and an even sounder investment in our services.

(Pause to let this sink in)…

"As an insider's secret, one of the key things to bear in mind is your emotional attachment to your home. As your independent advisor, we're emotionally unattached so emotions don't cloud our judgement when it comes to negotiating the best deal for you. It's simply a business deal. Again, in my experience I can tell you some horror stories of prospective clients who have attempted to go it alone and ended up getting their fingers burnt. Essentially, in negotiating, he who wants the deal the most, loses."

Then, list two or three examples of clients who got it wrong by trying to sell their property without your expert guidance, or with what they thought was a cheap/free online agent.

Someone recently shared on social media saying they sold their home "for free" via Strike, but by the time you added up all the costs of the 'additional marketing' they'd bought, it was actually more expensive than using a traditional agent.

"And let's be honest with one another, how high do you think your chances are of making a mistake in negotiating the sale price of your home when it's not your area of expertise? Especially if it's the first time you're doing this, your chances of making a mistake are very high. In my experience, most people aren't trained in the art of sales, so one simple mistake in this area can cost you thousands, if not tens of thousands, in the price you achieve for your home. Is it worth taking that risk? Especially when you could invest just 2% of the selling price to have us shoulder all the responsibility for you. And you already know we only get paid if we produce the goods…"

Some of these rebuttals might seem a little strong as pushbacks but this is vital to stop your clients from making what could be the most expensive mistake of their lives. You also need to show confidence in your skills and your service.

Ideally, you want to demonstrate your skills in situations where you've negotiated against other agents successfully by saying something along the lines of the following:

"Mr/s Client, I would just like to share with you a little story about negotiation which I think you'll find interesting. I was negotiating on behalf of a client recently in the sale of this home [show them an example], and the buyers instructed their own estate agent to negotiate with me on their behalf. The agent was a very tough negotiator and certainly talked a great game by telling me in no uncertain terms, that her client would only ever pay £35,000 less than the asking price for this property or they were going to walk away."

"Perhaps I could ask you Mr/s Client, what would you do as a homeowner in that situation?" See how they respond and take note of what feedback they give you. Then ask if they would like to know how you handled it. Assuming they say yes, proceed as follows:

"I simply asked the agent if she would kindly do me a favour. When she agreed, I said to her, would she be so kind as to call her clients and tell them that they've just lost the house of their dreams? She went very quiet on the other end of the phone for a few moments before telling me she would speak to them."

At this stage, I would tell the clients how the negotiating game sometimes relies upon nerves of steel and to buckle under the pressure of the negotiations, could cost them £10,000, £20,000 or in this case £35,000 on the sale of their home, particularly when a client has already found a home they want to move to. Some of you could be dealing with numbers closer to six figures which is a huge amount of money to be playing around with if potential clients mistakenly think they can negotiate a deal on their own.

"I'm pleased to report that within 20 minutes, I received a call from the agent saying their clients had "reluctantly" agreed to pay the asking price for the property. Now tell me, Mr/s client, can you see the value in having an expert agent like us with a ton of experience working on your behalf who knows how to bring negotiations to a successful conclusion for you? And can you see how achieving results similar to what I've just outlined, makes us worth every penny of our 2% fee?"

When they agree with you, ask them again for the business.

Here's another little secret share worth mentioning; throughout thousands of years of evolution, we've all learnt to communicate more or less through the use of stories. The greatest salesmen and women on the planet can help clients see their point of view by outlining it with a story of some sort which makes what they're saying far more memorable. Therefore, take the time to craft stories around your rebuttals so they convey the points you want to make to your clients when you're overcoming their objections.

As Drew Eric Whitman, marketing Guru, says: "Think about it. How do most salespeople train for their jobs? They simply read up on their products, learn a little about their market (or not), shadow a current employee (often not the best one), and then go out and try their utmost to persuade people to buy. The majority use "lay" methodology and usually get mediocre results."

So, take the time to study your clients, work up rebuttals to common objections and share stories as examples to get your points across.

Objection #3:

"I'm definitely going to do this, now just isn't the right time."

"I have a lot going on in my life right now; it's just not the right time"

"My son/daughter is going through university/exams, and I don't want to disrupt that"

"I'm really busy at work/business and I don't have time to do this right now."

Rebuttal:

"Let's be honest about this, have you ever had a time when life was 'just right'? You know, when you wanted to do something with no other distractions in your life such as work, kids, financial worries etc? No? Why? Because it doesn't happen! This thing called 'life' always gets in the way so there will never be a time when all your ducks are in a row. What it comes down to is making this a priority in your life."

"Can I ask you something? Why do you want to sell your property? What are you really trying to achieve?" If you recall, you asked these questions at the start of the market appraisal visit and so you should see if the answers you get now match the ones the client gave before. Re-explore their objectives and try to uncover their pain points (not enough space, financial pressures, takes too long to get to work, etc.), or dig deeper to uncover the real reasons behind what they're trying to achieve.

"The market conditions we have right now are where the big money will be made and are unlikely to be repeated again in our lifetimes – why would you want to miss out on such a great opportunity? Procrastination will not help you achieve the best price for your home. The 2008 credit crunch taught us that the market can change by 20-40% almost overnight! Can you really afford to miss out on achieving such a great price for your home?"

Objection #4

"I've got another agent coming to look at the property later/next week and I need to see them before I can make my decision."

Rebuttal

"Thank you for sharing that with me. Can I ask, is there a particular reason why you're thinking about using the other agent? What is it that you're hoping to get from them that we haven't already covered here today?"

This is particularly important as you want to know if there's an existing relationship with the other agent; do they know them personally, or are your competition doing something you're not aware of, which makes potential clients very keen to want to work with them?

After they answer, take some notes, and then push back against their objection along the lines of the following:

"Ok great, so I understand that you want to see XYZ agent for the following reasons (list them), and are those the only reasons? I'm merely asking for market research purposes, and who better to ask than our potential clients, right? Clearly if we're missing a trick, as an agent at the top of our game, we want to know what it is!" Keep it light-hearted.

They'll hopefully dive a little deeper into the information they've given you or perhaps reveal something you didn't know. If it's a personal relationship or friendship of some sort, ask them outright if there's any possibility of winning the business or have they already made their mind up to use them. This is not to be short with them, but to avoid wasting your time so you can move onto more serious clients if you suspect they're tyre-kickers, or you're being used as a yardstick, (or worse, they're 'shopping you' for their agent friend).

If they've got an unusual home, or there's something else driving the need to ask other agents to value their property, you may have to agree to align yourself with them, before directing the conversation down an avenue that you prefer.

For example, you could say something like:

"Fantastic! Thanks for sharing that with me. Of course, with a property such as this, I don't blame you for asking other agents to look at it. You want to be sure that you're making the right decision. And in order to help you, if you haven't already seen this, I would like to give you a complimentary copy of our 'Ultimate Guide To Choosing The Best Agent To Help Sell Your Home' (or similar title giveaway), which independently reviews the key factors you should take into account. I hope you'll forgive me when I bashfully tell you that we, of course, meet all the relevant criteria..."

Rather than leaving your client punch-drunk from a barrage of reasons why they should use, you, provide some memorable value instead from a resource designed to truly help them (and not just be a sales pitch for your company). You'll also find some of the following closing techniques useful to overcome objections and help you close the deal.

Finally, you could use this as an opportunity to increase scarcity and desire by referring to the number of available spaces you have for each of your packages, or the fact that key bonus they really want will be going away as you're ending that promotion very soon.

You may be able to hold it open for 24 hours, but after that, you're sorry there's nothing more you can do. This focusses their mind and gets you back in the driving seat with your presentation.

If you want to know how you can really add value to your clients and your business, there's a ton of extra resources we can share with you on a call.

We just ask you to invest 30 minutes into a complimentary consultation, where we can help fast-track your success (with no hard sell whatsoever).

Here's the link to book your call:

http://www.wiggywam.co.uk/estateagentssecretscall

CHAPTER ELEVEN

SECRET CLOSING TECHNIQUES

What follows are some of the most powerful secret closing techniques we've learnt in our professional career in sales and the property industry so far.

Use these techniques with caution and always remember, it's all about genuinely helping people, not just about winning business. If you can't help them, have the moral integrity to turn them away or refer them to someone who can.

The Performance-Based Approach

If a client feels their property deserves to be marketed at a higher price than you genuinely feel it's worth, why not make a game out of it and incentivise your performance? For example, let's say you've valued the property at £400,000 and they seem to think it's worth £425,000, you can say the fairest way to deal with it is you're prepared to have a go at achieving the higher figure, but because of the extra time, effort and work that will be involved, you'll have to charge a fee that's incentivised in your favour.

For example, let's say your standard fee is 1.5% and you'd be happy to charge that if they agree to market it at £400,000. If you were to achieve £410,000+, you want 2%, reducing to 1.5% on any offer they accept at £410,000 or less.

Bear in mind it doesn't just have to be based on straight-forward percentages. You could agree 1.5% up to £400,000 and then 10% of any figure over that. If they accepted £415,000 for example, (and the sale went through), you'd get your 1.5% on the £400,000 (£6,000) and then 10% of the £15,000 (£1,500) which is much better than 1.5% on the total sale price.

From a negotiation standpoint, this allows you some flexibility to move up and down the fee scale. If they don't agree to the 2% on the whole amount, using performance-based fees over a certain threshold, can help both you and your client meet in the middle, and give them the feeling they've won. This is especially true if you're dealing with a driver, sociable or analytical type personalities.

The Take-Away

This is one of the most powerful secret objection-handling responses you can use when dealing with prospective clients. When you try to take something away from people, they always seem to want it more! It's a strange psychological phenomenon, but it's true! Think about how much your desire to go to a certain restaurant increases, when it's difficult to get a table. If you do finally get a table, you automatically feel pretty special.

It's the same with agency. When you know what you're worth, and you know you do a really good job for your clients, you don't have to chase everyone for their business. Refusing to do business with people, or restricting the opportunity to work with you, can make them want you more. So, you might want to say something along the lines of the following:

"Mr/s Client, I want you to know that I respect your thoughts on the price you feel the property ought to be advertised at. It's your home, so ultimately, you call the shots. However, as I'm sure you can appreciate, our business relies on us taking properties to the market that are realistically priced so we can sell them and help our clients achieve their objectives, similarly to the ones you've outlined that are important to you, such as X, Y & Z" (list their objectives).

"I do like your property, and it would be our pleasure to market it for you at the price of £X (your valuation figure), however in my professional opinion, having sold X number of similar homes in this area over the last few years I do feel that a price of £Y (their figure), is not achievable. As I want to do the very best job I can for my clients, on this occasion, I cannot take the property to the market at the higher price as ultimately, I would be doing you a great disservice."

"I do not want you to have to go through weeks or months of frustration because your property hasn't sold, despite our best efforts to try and find you a buyer. As you probably know, moving home is the third most stressful thing we do in life, and we don't want to compound that stress by putting you in a position where you've lost your dream home, because we couldn't sell this one in time. It would be unprofessional of me to do so and I am sure you can appreciate my position when I say that on this occasion, at the higher figure, I'll have to decline to market it for you."

Now at this point, your client may feel an element of rejection, so notice any change in their body language. Folded arms, flushing of the cheeks, a change in the energy of the room, or tonality of their voice, can all indicate your client may have taken your comments a little more personally than they ought to. You may wish to soften the blow by saying something along the lines of:

"I hope you'll appreciate it's nothing personal and if you'll permit me to, I'd like to share some examples of other clients that found themselves in a situation similar to yours."

You've put the client on the back foot slightly, then given them a chance to save face and allow yourself to gain their trust by showing them you have their best interests at heart. Show them examples of other properties that were on the market with your competition which had been overvalued and didn't sell. Show them your valuation and the date you looked at the property, the date it went on the market with your competitor and at what price, how long it was on the market for, when you took control of it, and the price you sold it for. The more examples, the better as this gives your client the reassurance they need.

If you have testimonials you can share at this point, even better. Especially if they demonstrate your client's journey and how they endured months of frustration by trying to get a higher price, before switching to you who got the job done at the price you originally suggested. Not enough agents take the time to do this, and it can be very persuasive to your clients when you do this effectively (without bad-mouthing your competition).

Incidentally, a top-secret tip on gathering testimonials. If you just give a client a blank brief and ask them for a testimonial, chances are, they either won't do it, or they'll say a few things, which may not meet your marketing needs.

One secret is to write the testimonial for them and ask them if they agree with it or not. Get them to agree in writing with the commentary, and say you can use it for marketing, and away you go.

Take the time to go through these examples of your experience. Ask your clients if they want to face similar troubling circumstances where they must endure months of frustration waiting around trying to find a buyer, or face losing the home they had their eyes on because of a poor choice in the marketing price of the property.

Tell them that one of the most frequently overlooked things when it comes to selling homes (especially empty ones), is the 'hidden costs' involved by having to pay the mortgage. If their mortgage is £1,000 a month, and they waste 6 months or more on the market without selling, this can easily add up to £6,000+ council tax and other bills. They need to consider all this when deciding on the price, as well as their willingness to accept any offers.

Most prospects are reasonable and will agree with you. Others not so. Those that won't see sense are best left to their own devices and you can be there for them in the future, if, as, and when they come to their senses.

CHAPTER TWELVE

SECRETS TO BUILDING YOUR DREAM TEAM

"The most important decisions that business people make are not <u>what</u> decisions, but <u>who</u> decisions." Jim Collins, author of Good to Great.

We know we've covered a lot so far, so you're forgiven if you're feeling a little overwhelmed. Most business owners are usually stacked out with work every day, and sometimes over the weekend too. So, when they read a book like this, which shares ideas on how to improve their service level offering, the natural reaction is to procrastinate by saying something to the effect of "I'll do this later…"

Of course, later never comes and the precious gemstones of wisdom trapped between the pages of this book begin to gather dust on the shelf, waiting for some eager entrepreneur to unearth them and claim the rewards.

If you're serious about putting this into action, one of the hidden secrets is not to try and do this all by yourself. You're going to need to hire a crack team of 'A' players to bring your vision to life. And before your inner voice complains that such hires are incredibly expensive, be patient as we share more on how to find the right people for you and your business.

As Simon Sinek says: "If you hire people just because they can do a job, they'll work for money…but if you hire people who believe what you believe, they'll work for you with blood, sweat and tears." This is one of the reasons why we focused on culture in Volume I by establishing your values, so you have a clear target to aim for in your hiring process.

The mistake most business owners make is to delay the hiring process (because they think they can't afford it), until they're overloaded with work and then simply grab the first person who comes along with a pulse! The new hire shadows one or two people in the office for a few weeks (who are also extremely busy so can't really invest the time in doing a good job of the training), and then they're set loose on clients... what could possibly go wrong?!

So, as an incentive to get the hiring process right, in the book Topgrading, it's been suggested that the cost of a bad hire is 15 times their annual salary. If they're earning the highest bracket of minimum wage, (around £25,000), that's still an enormous cost to your business if you get this wrong. The trouble is, most business owners don't realise that cost as the money hasn't come directly out of their bank account. But what happens to all the time, effort and expense invested into the hiring process? Does it simply evaporate? Well, to a certain extent, yes, but if you get a particularly bad hire, it could do irrevocable damage to your business and its reputation.

Your key focus should be to attract and hire A players into our business; the type of people who are self-starting, motivated, committed, and who want to take pride in a job well done. But we also want to have a little variety in our business by working with people who are not just clones of us.

As you saw in the personality profiling section of Volume I, if you're dealing with the general public, you're going to meet people from all walks of life and all personality types across the spectrum. Having people with different personalities working in your office is going to help build rapid rapport with more potential clients, increasing your chance of winning more business.

Before we get into the nitty-gritty of the hiring process, a secret hack here is to start building a 'subs bench' for your business. Any professional sports team has a subs bench which includes various of players who can drop into the right position if another player is out due to injury, suspension or they leave the team.

In your case, you're going to be building a virtual subs bench, where you identify potential hires in the marketplace who you would like to work with, and who could be very valuable to you. You'll then earmark them for future positions in your business.

As an example, let's say you go to a local restaurant, and you receive outstanding customer service from a waiter or waitress and you can't help but think they'd make a great addition to your team. You could pass them your business card and ask them to get in touch, explaining that you don't have a position available yet, but you could make one available soon if they're interested. We know two partners at a law firm who managed to find some stellar staff in McDonald's of all places! So always be on the lookout for the right people.

The same can apply for those you meet who may currently be in the employ of one of your competitors. Whilst you might feel uncomfortable poaching them, what about casually asking them if they have any plans to move on in a year or two? Tell them you'd be very keen to hear from them if they did decide to make a change.

The point is, you're building up a pipeline of potential 'substitutes' who you can bring into your business if, God forbid, one or more of your staff members is unable to work due to sickness, pregnancy, bereavement, or they simply decide to leave. This immediately removes any pressure you may feel if such a situation happens, or you feel the crushing burden of having to go through the hiring process to find someone fast, with all the inherent risks of getting it wrong.

Even better, you get to keep more cash in your pocket which you're not having to fork out to recruitment agents (who vary in quality substantially). Our own experience many years ago of being the subject of recruitment companies was in reaching out to five different firms in Birmingham. Two asked us to fill out a form, four we never heard from again, and only one agent took the time to hold an interview, find out a lot more information about us and within an hour of leaving, she had two interviews lined up the very next day. Needless to say, some are worth their weight in gold whilst others are just in it for the easy money.

Paying Staff To Leave

This might seem like a strange concept, but sometimes a big secret is to pay staff to leave if they're not the right fit for your business or you're not sure of their motives for working at your company. Amazon has used a 'Pay to Quit' policy for some time where they offer a cash incentive to leave if the staff feel it's not the right fit for them.

Leaving bonuses at Amazon start at $2,000 and go up a grand a year to a maximum of $5,000. Despite this appearing like a backwards way to retain staff, in Bezos's own words he wants; "to encourage folks to take a moment and think about what they really want. In the long run, an employee staying somewhere they don't want to be isn't healthy for the employee or the company."

Think about the rational for having such a policy – whilst it might seem like a big lump of cash to give away to be left with the problem of having one less person in your company, the impact on your business of having an uninspired employee whose clock watching all day is not going to help you get to where you want to be. And whilst its true Amazon is a cash rich company who can afford to offer this, is there something in this which can add value to your business to help retain staff for the long term?

So, take the pressure off by not working with those who are only in it for the wage, build your subs bench, and bring in the top A players you can find to self-manage and share the burden of working on your business with you. We would go so far as to say a good A player is worth at least two clock-watchers and will require much less of your time to manage.

The Job Scorecard

How do you conduct your hiring process?

If you're like most business owners, the temptation is, (because they're so busy and just need someone to fill the position NOW), to do a 'feel good' interview where they essentially sit down with the potential new hire, have a chat centred loosely around the job, their prior work experience, and any relevant qualifications. Then, they make the hire based on the candidate they felt they got on the best with, or worse, who's available to start asap!

The best hiring method would be based on prior experience of working with the potential candidate, so you have some idea of their strengths and weaknesses and can make a more informed decision. That may not be possible, or you may have already used this method of hiring and quickly exhausted the list of potential candidates who would make good hires.

One secret is to offer them 'work experience' at your organisation for a short period, ideally at least 2-4 weeks. This can work to both party's advantage. When we were struggling to find an opening as an estate agent many years ago, we simply offered to work there for a month, for free. Not only did this show commitment, but it also meant the manager could see whether we were a good fit for the business, and if not, at least we now had the benefit of some work experience to show on the CV. It worked amazingly well because who in their right mind offers to work for free...? And who in their right mind would turn someone down who made such an offer...? Can you see how making offers so good people would feel stupid saying no works in all areas of life?

If that's not possible, or feasible, the next secret is to create a job scorecard for the position you want to hire for, rather than a job description, and use the scorecard in the hiring process. The scorecard details a person's purpose for the role, the desired outcomes you want them to achieve, and the competencies (both technical and cultural) required to execute their position.

According to Brad Smart, author of the book Topgrading, such a system hits a 90% success rate for finding the right hire, as opposed to the 25-60% success rate using the process we touched on earlier.

A key component of the job scorecard is to identify a handful of <u>specific</u> and <u>measurable</u> outcomes which you feel the person hired for this position will need to accomplish over the next 1-3 years. It describes, in tangible detail (which helps hugely during quarterly, six-monthly, and annual reviews), the outcomes you want them to achieve from their activities in the role. Whilst it's important to be realistic, the outcomes ought to be a stretch for the new hire to achieve. An A Player will want to rise to the challenge of exceeding the requirements for the position to show you they're the right man, or woman, for the job. Tie in a bonus structure which recognises their over performance, and you're in business.

By detailing some specific outcomes, you require, you're bringing logic and structure to the hiring process, as you're evaluating <u>all</u> potential candidates against the same criteria, not just whether you like them or not, or you get 'a really good feeling about this one...'

Put simply, during the interview process, do you really feel they can deliver the results you want, and have they achieved similar outcomes in their previous roles, or will this be their first attempt? Is their job with you going to be on a trial basis against measurable outcomes you want them to achieve within the first 90 days? Building such structure will quickly sift the wheat from the chaff so it's likely any bad hire will leave quickly if they're not hitting the targets you've set.

Finally, do you honestly feel they'll be a good fit within your company culture? Will they integrate seamlessly alongside the rest of the team, or will they become disruptive? You don't just want 'yes men' (or women), so a little friction is not a bad thing, but too much may upset your best team members causing them to leave, putting you further behind than when you started.

As an example, working in a city centre surveying practice, we experienced an intolerable situation. The office partner was a super guy to work with and we respected him hugely. Yet for some strange reason, one of the managers who worked under him was a particularly contemptible person. Not only was he arrogant (without good reason to be), his aggressive nature and dictating ways rubbed everyone in the office up the wrong way (apart from the partner of course!).

Worse, he was the weak kind of beta-male who would give out grief to others in the office, but if you gave a bit back and made others laugh at his expense, he HATED it.

After being at the company for only a few weeks, because of his attitude, we made up our minds we would leave the moment we were qualified. The irony of the story was, a few weeks prior to leaving, the office staff attended a professional development lecture by the author of the book 'Multipliers' (Liz Wiseman) who explained how employees left companies because of bad managers. Think about all the time, effort and energy devoted to training a surveyor and building a team, only to have them leave because of an obnoxious and foolish manager.

Once we'd handed our notice in, he didn't speak to us for the entire month, until on the day of leaving, he barked "Boardroom now!" and unleashed a tidal wave of abuse making it very clear what he thought. This was his encouragement for us to stay with the company!! Not only did it fail to work, but as the market entered a recession a few months later, he was promptly fired.

Who Is An 'A' Player

The definition of an A player is "someone in the top 10% of the available talent pool who is willing to accept your specific offer." Note this definition does not mean hiring the best of the best and paying an unreasonable amount for such a person. Leave that hiring strategy to the banks! You're interested in bagging those individuals who have a strong work ethic and who are available at the salary and compensation you can realistically offer. Essentially, you're sorting the wheat from the chaff to uncover the one-in-ten-star player who's going to add some serious value to your business, and not be a drain on your resources.

You know the type of people we're talking about as you've no doubt met them in different jobs and professions. They're smart, efficient, friendly, eager to please, and with a strong work ethic that simply gets the job done, no matter what it takes. They'll also do their best to remove as many hurdles as possible to help you. Ever had stellar service at a four or five-star hotel or restaurant? Or been to an independent shop where the owner was super keen to help you? Did it literally bring a smile to your soul to be treated this way?

You also know the difference between poor-quality staff who are disinterested, dull, can't really be bothered, and who will try to put barriers in your way rather than helping you or your clients. And if you don't know, start to take notice of how people treat you when you're a consumer of products and services. Ever tried contacting your local authority, major multi-national company or even your bank...? What's your experience like?

How Do We Find Them?

When designing your hiring process, ask yourself the following questions:

1. How can we expect our employees to be extraordinary and differentiate our company if we use the same hiring and onboarding methods as our competitors?

2. What characteristics describe our ideal team which our competitors could not or would not use to describe theirs?

Apart from building out the job scorecard (more on that in a moment), the way you conduct the interview process will also likely change. The top talent won't accept a lack of challenge in the hiring process and will be eager to prove they're the best at what they do. If the hiring process is too easy, they'll likely lose respect for your organisation and not be tempted to work there, even if you offer them a job.

By increasing the length of the interview process, you're going to stack the following in your favour:

1. Easily expose the "professional interviewees" who cannot maintain a façade for 3-4 hours when hiring management or C-suite execs (1-2 hours for 'regular' employees).

2. Those who are initially nervous in the interview will have the time to relax and get into their flow – important so they can show you more of who they really are.

3. The true star players will feel as though you have taken the interview process seriously and dedicated sufficient time to it to make it rigorous enough for them to shine a spotlight on their capabilities.

4. Isn't investing 1-4 hours into the interview process to find the right person, (or avoid the wrong one), better than getting it wrong and having to go through the whole process again a short time later on whilst having to mop up the aftermath (and costs), of getting the wrong hire in your business?

Check References

As you're building out your interviewing process, a top secret is to go through the candidate's entire work history and ask questions about whom they reported to at each role, including clarifying the spelling of each boss's name (and be seen to write it all down), to show you're serious about checking references. Ask what each boss will say about them <u>when</u> you call them.

The threat of a reference check quickly uncovers any candidate trying to 'blag it' in the interview, or who may have left a company on unfavourable terms. A good indication of an A Player will be their willingness to arrange phone calls with their previous bosses, or at least notify them to expect your call.

And be careful not to judge too quickly if an employee left on unfavourable terms – what if the company culture was one of dishonesty and they refused to go along with it? Does that make them a bad person even though their previous boss may hate them because they threatened to expose the wrongdoings?

What Questions Do I Ask?

Here's some questions you can ask to establish work ethic and get to know the candidate:

1. Did they have a part-time job growing up? If so, ask them to tell you more about it.
2. What did they spend money on as a teenager? And how did they get that money?
3. Do they discuss religion or politics with people? When was their last passionate debate? Who was it with? And what was it about? How did it turn out?
4. What are the values they hold dear to them? Can they give you some examples of how they've applied those values in their life? Can they give you some examples of how they applied those values to a situation which had a less than favourable outcome for them?
5. What was the last thing they learnt?
6. How often do they read? What type of books do they like to read? What was the last book they read?

7. How do they like to receive feedback or criticism? Are they a take it on the chin person, or someone who needs a little more diplomacy?
8. How do they deliver criticism or feedback to a co-worker? And to a more senior colleague?
9. What's their biggest passion? What do they love doing more than anything?
10. What companies do they admire? And why?
11. Why are they interested in working at your company?

Ask them to walk you through their work experience and career history. Get them to tell you all about each position, starting with the first job they got. Who was the manager? What do you think their manager will say about them when you call them?

Once they've gone through one job or position, move onto the next. Build out a timeline of all the different jobs or positions they've had and see if there's any gaps in their employment history. Probe further to find out why.

How do they feel about working towards the objectives you've identified as essential for this role? Have they worked under such conditions before, or will this be their first time? Dig a little deeper on any references they've provided – how do they know them? And again, what will they say about them?

Key Criteria

You've probably heard the phrase, "Hire for attitude, train for skills" and we couldn't agree more. Focus on these four secret things when hiring new employees:

1. Their Will – their desire to excel at what they do, to take action with courage, to persevere, an expression of their desire to learn and a need to innovate. (But can you let go of the reigns long enough to allow them to truly shine?).
2. Their Values – do their own values align with the core values of your company? (Hopefully you can now see why you took the time to establish your mission, vision, and values in Volume I).

3. The Results You Want – Do you honestly believe they can deliver the outcomes, critical drivers, or KPI's you've identified to fulfil this position? Or are you just desperate enough to grab the first person who comes along?

4. Their Skills – Hire for attitude, train for skills. Almost all skills can be taught to the right person with the right attitude. A bad attitude will leave you and your clients frustrated.

When you hire the right people, you're making your life easier because they'll get on and do the right work for years to come, but the wrong ones will create headaches and problems for you which will take time, effort, energy, and potentially (big) sums of money to put right.

Managing the hiring process against your culture, values, and mission, offers more to people than just a job. You're offering a family or community of people who think like they think and believe what they believe. And that's good for them as well as you, because the right fit will feel at home, embody your values, deliver the service you want to deliver with passion, and won't be clock-watching waiting on the next pay rise, or worse, using your company as a stepping-stone.

An Outline Of The Job Scorecard

The secret of the job scorecard is that it can make the biggest difference to your hiring process. So, let's look at the component parts we can use to flush out A players:

Measurable Outcomes: You must tie performance of the role to 3-8 tangible outcomes, by order of importance, which someone working in this position can achieve. Without measurable outcomes, performance reviews become an unfair exercise for both parties. Any performance review should always tie back to these measurables. Are they hitting them or not? And if not, what can be done about it, if anything? We're all 'busy' during the workday, but busy doing what? Are your staff productive, or merely treading water 'doing their email' until closing time? Productive staff will have an eye on their targets and what they need to do to achieve them.

For example, is one of your measurable outcomes a valuation to new instruction rate of 40%? Firstly, is that the right outcome for the position you're hiring for (accounts or admin versus a valuer/lister), and secondly, is it achievable in the local area? Ideally, you should have no more than three measurable outcomes for each position.

More importantly, any employee who has been set measurable outcomes who isn't hitting them, likely knows it and will take appropriate action (step up or leave) before they're fired. It gives greater transparency on the hiring and firing process. It helps to have a robust and measurable tracking process in place against as many of the measurable outcomes as possible, so you're not measuring performance by sticking a finger in the air and deciding which way the wind's blowing. It's against factual data – did they hit these targets or not?

When outcomes are clear, it creates a natural filtering process for who will apply and who won't, because who wants to apply for a role they feel they're automatically going to fail at? No one. That said, outcomes need to be a stretch, yet also realistic.

For example, if the top-performing 'A' player valuer in your area can close £150,000 of fees per year, your targets should be in this region, and not £300,000. Also, by defining just the outcomes, and not the daily habits they'll need to use (calling customers for example), you give more freedom for someone to use their initiative to achieve the results you're asking for. They might decide to cold call 1,000 people or write a direct-response letter. You're not as invested in the <u>process</u> as you are the <u>outcome</u>. Does that make sense? Besides, trying to dictate to 'A' players is not the best strategy. Flush them out in the hiring process, give them a framework to work within, tie it to the desired outcome and then set them loose!

Mission Statement: Does it sound a little weird having a mission statement for a job role? Not at all. If the company has an overall mission (which you also established in Volume I), then its only right employees have individual ones too – naturally their missions should align with the overall mission of the company.

The mission statement is a broader description of what the role will entail (ideally no more than 4-6 lines – keep it concise), as an overview, with the measurable outcomes giving more detail in key areas.

Key Competencies: Here you're looking at matching the key competencies of the organisation with those of the individual. In other words, is there a cultural fit or will there be a culture clash? As long as the candidate has a willingness to learn, the cultural fit is far more valuable than their skills (unless it's a specifically technically role, such as a coder).

Hopefully you can see why we asked you to establish your core values in Volume I. Alignment here is crucial if you don't want to be on the endless treadmill to nowhere of hiring and firing staff who don't fit into your company culture.

If you're struggling to understand your company culture, simply gather the leadership team together and ask: "What words would we use to describe our culture?" and write down everything that comes up. You'll soon start to see a pattern emerging which will give you deeper insight into what your company culture is all about. Be honest here however – we all want to be part of an exciting and dynamic organisation, but does that really apply if it takes a week to reply to letters or emails? Defining where you are and where you'd like to get to are the keys to this task.

More importantly, if you do somehow succeed in luring 'A-players into your company by doing a great selling job on your culture and they arrive to find out it's not as you describe, one of two things is going to happen. They'll immediately leave, or they'll dive headlong into making the company reflect the culture you sold them on because that's their values. And that could make the other team members uncomfortable, or worse, resistant, increasing the chances your star player will leave, or you'll face mutiny from your existing staff.

To help you out, here's a list of competencies to consider when hiring 'A' players:

Efficiency: You want your staff to be as efficient as possible in achieving their outcomes. Can they hit those measurable outcomes with minimal wasted effort?

Honesty & Integrity: We're sure you'll agree this is vital as a character trait. You want honesty and integrity in your staff – can they be relied upon or are you going to have an uphill battle in determining the truth with what they're telling you? Fudging numbers and results makes it impossible to run a business. Transparency is key.

Planning & Organisation: Do they have the ability to plan effectively and focus on the key priorities necessary to get the job done?

Aggressiveness: Can they move quickly towards their outcomes, and do they have the backbone required to make it happen? Importantly, in a people-facing role, can they do it without coming across as rubbing others up the wrong way?

Keep their commitments: Are they keeping the commitments they make to your clients? No matter if those agreements require them to work late or weekends to meet them?

Intelligence: Can they learn quickly and take in new information at the rate required for the modern world?

Analytical Skills: Are they the type of person to dive beneath the surface to unearth new insights or do they take everything at face value?

Attention to Detail: Are they bright & responsible enough to effectively manage their projects and responsibilities without letting things slip which could undermine everything they're working on?

Persistence: Will they go the extra mile (especially in the face of defeat)?

Proactivity: Do you feel they can be self-sufficient and autonomous with their actions and bring new things to the table, or are they going to be reliant on everyone else (or you)?

The above list reflects the core competencies you should be looking for in all your A-player hires. The following is a list of others that could be useful, depending on the role:

Teamwork: Can they work cohesively as part of a team environment, or are they a lone wolf? The ability to collaborate is important, as is the ability to integrate in the team without rubbing people up the wrong way.

Chemistry: Do they have the level of personal chemistry required to work with your clients and team?

Coachability: Will they be coachable in their role, or do you get the impression they think they already know everything?

Communication: Are they able to communicate well with the written and spoken word? More importantly, can they listen?

Ego Under Wraps: Nobody likes a braggard, or someone who's so arrogant you can't get through to them. For some roles, a bit of ego is essential, but the ability to set it aside and offer up a genuine apology is also necessary.

Persuasion: Can they convince clients and/or the team to move in a certain direction or follow a course of action?

Calm Under Pressure: Are they able to be calm under pressure, especially with the stresses of the job, or will they exhibit erratic or irrational behaviour when the stakes are high? Or worse, take time off when the pressure sets in?

Adaptability: Are they flexible enough to change with the demanding day-to-day circumstances of business life or will they remain stuck in their ways?

Strategic Thinking: Can they grasp the big picture and, more importantly, communicate this to others, with enthusiasm? And do they have their finger on the pulse of the ever-changing business environment and current trends which could affect the company?

Innovative: Can they come up with new solutions to old problems? Or figure out ways to eliminate those problems altogether?

High Standards: Do they expect the best from themselves and their team and do they have the skillset to achieve those standards?

Open to Feedback: Nobody likes to be criticised, but can they actively seek out feedback from their team and superiors, even if its negative? And will they calmly take it on board, or will they become hostile and push back?

Enthusiasm: Are they passionate and excited about their work? And do they have a 'get-it-done' attitude?

For managerial positions:

Ability to Hire A-players: Can they sift the wheat from the chaff to find, interview, select and hire the right A-players to join the business?

Ability to Develop People: Can they coach and build people up in their current roles to improve overall performance? Can they identify the right candidates to train up for superior positions, even if it threatens their own job?

What Does a Job Scorecard Look Like?

Curiosity is a powerful thing, so let's look at a template job scorecard for a valuer or lister within an estate agency to see how this would come together:

Valuer Job Scorecard			
Position: Any Co. Estate agency valuer **Location:** Berkshire			
Core Mission: The core mission of the Any Co. Estate agency valuer is to increase revenue to the business from new and existing customers, through effectively selling the agency services of Any Co. to those clients who want to move home. Contact will be through telephone, email, online chat/forums, WiggyWam marketplace, and face-to-face meetings and valuers are expected to be innovative in their approach to finding new ways to gain new clients and win their business.			
Accountabilities	Metric	Rating (A, B, C)	Comments
Generate Revenue	£20,000 per month within 12 weeks. £50,000 per month within 52 weeks.		
Average	£2,500 per month		

Commission	within 12 weeks.		
Client Volume	6 clients per month within 12 weeks. 12 clients per month within 52 weeks.		
Activity	Attend 20 valuations per month. Leaflet drop 100 houses per week. Call 100 local prospects per week.		
Reporting	Complete & submit daily activity sheets. Send all client reports within 48 hours.		

Key Competencies:

- Coachability   - Enthusiasm
- Personal Chemistry   - Calm under pressure
- Integrity   - Teamwork
- Strong work ethic   - Persistence

When you take the time to produce a Job Scorecard for each role, you'll save yourself a ton of time, stress, and frustration in the hiring process. Can you see how measurable these accountabilities are? And how they offer an opportunity for improvement, and setting new ones as the market changes, or working practices alter which provide improve results?

The ability to promote or coach at each performance review then becomes available and all candidates have full transparency of the entire hiring and firing process.

Finally, the job scorecard should be an organic document which evolves over time and is not static or fixed in stone.

The Most Overlooked Secret Of Hiring New People

As you've gone through Volumes I & II so far, the 'method in the madness' has begun to become clear. So, let's give you a bit of an 'Ah-ha' moment as we pull another earlier learning into this section.

Earlier on, we talked about the importance of knowing the numbers in your business, if you're going to be successful. And whilst this is vital to navigate and pilot your company, the most overlooked secret of hiring new people is tying accountability & responsibility for the numbers back to each individual role.

Confused? Let's spell it out for you…

Every staff member has a specific role they do within the company. But not many people realise how their individual performance affects the overall running of the company or more specifically, its financial performance. To remover this uncertainty, you want to tie part of their measurable outcomes to each line of the accounts or financial statements of your business.

For example, salespeople will naturally drive revenue. So, part of their measurable outcomes should reflect accountability for the revenue section of the financial statements. If you have three salespeople who all have the measurable outcome of driving £300,000 of fee income into the company per year, they're each <u>responsible</u> for contributing one-third of the top-line revenue i.e., £100,000.

Collectively, they're <u>accountable</u> for the £300,000 of revenue the sales team should be bringing in this year.

This provides tangibility and transparency to the numbers and allows all parties to track performance throughout the year against these measurables. £300,000 a year revenue translates to £25,000 a month or £8,333.33 per salesperson. As each month unfolds, you can see if the team, and each individual, is on track to do their numbers, and if they're not, you can intervene early rather than waiting until the end of the financial year (like most businesses), to find out they haven't hit target. More importantly, each staff member knows whether they're on track or not, and if one is struggling, they can seek assistance, coaching, or mentoring earlier on before the situation gets out of hand.

The secret to this system is that every position has transparency and accountability. With careful thought, the overall financial targets can be translated into measurable outcomes for each individual team, and drilled down further into each individual role's accountabilities:

Financial Targets ➜ Team Responsibilities ➜ Individual Accountabilities

Does this make more sense now? Once you grasp the importance of this, your whole organisation can change, if you take action and implement it.

Finally, if you're going to implement this into your organisation, have the discipline to pass over talented people if they're not a great fit for you. Whilst it can be tempting to hire them in the heat of the moment, it can put you back to square one if they get ejected by the team or leave as they feel too uncomfortable being there.

CONCLUSION

Congratulations on making it to the end of Volume II. You're now standing on the precipice of being able to make a dramatic difference to your business through applying all you've learnt so far and building on this knowledge using the final secrets in Volume III - Execute.

This is a truly exciting time, and one which is full of hope and promise, but which can equally slip away and become forgotten unless you take action on what you've learnt so far and complete all your learnings through to the end of the trilogy.

It can be difficult implementing this roadmap, especially with all the day-to-day pressures of business and the constant interruptions you face. This is what stops most business owners from ever making the changes they need to, leaving them frustrated and out of pocket.

Our ultimate goal from this book series is to ensure you succeed in your business, and we're happy to help you as much as possible.

We offer an exclusive 12-week training program, dedicated to support you in implementing each and every step of the roadmap in your business, and getting you the results you deserve.

If you'd like to know more, the first step is to book in a complimentary 30-minute consultation, so we can find out more about your goals and dreams, and how we can help you get there as quickly as possible.

Here's the link to book the call:

http://www.wiggywam.co.uk/estateagentssecretscall

ADDITIONAL SECRET RESOURCES

If you're the type of person who values learning, we've pulled together some great resources that can really help you to implement a lot of the things we've talked about in this book. Here's a list of some of the things we think you'll find helpful.

Read the following books:

1) The psychology of selling by Brian Tracy
2) The one-minute sales person by Spencer Johnson
3) Purple Cow by Seth Godin
4) Expert Secrets Trilogy by Russell Brunson
5) Brain Scripts by Drew Eric Whitman
6) Ca$hvertising by Drew Eric Whitman
7) Topgrading by Bradford D. Smart
8) Who by Geoff Smart and Randy Street
9) Scaling Up by Verne Harnish
10) Estate Agents Secrets Trilogy by Silas J. Lees - http://www.wiggywam.co.uk/estateagentssecretstrilogy

ABOUT THE AUTHOR

Silas is the author of a number of property related books including the Estate Agent's Secrets Trilogy, and As Safe As Houses – Cracking The Code To Profitable Property Investment. He also explores the more spiritual side of life in his book – Love Is The New Religion.

As someone who has been in property all his life, he's passionate about using his decades of experience to improve the home buying, selling, and renting journey, to help everyone involved.

Despite working in the family business from the age of 9, Silas's first real job was as an estate agent, and he fell in love with the industry at 18. He then trained to become a Building Surveyor to understand property at a deeper level, before going on to become a property investor in 2007, buying his first buy-to-let property about 5 minutes before the credit crunch recession gripped the UK!

Despite these setbacks and challenges, he went on to build a respectable property portfolio before training others how to replicate his success working alongside such household names as Martin Roberts from Homes Under The Hammer, Robbie Fowler (the footballer), and internationally renowned author Robert Kiyosaki.

Frustrated at the length of time it takes to buy and sell for most people and having bought and sold homes in days as an investor, Silas turned his attention to doing something about changing the way the UK housing market works.

This led him to start WiggyWam – the UK's first property platform built as a collaborative communication bridge between estate agents and lawyers, to get deals done far more quickly.

WiggyWam's mission is to remove the barriers people face when moving home and the company is constantly on the lookout for collaborative opportunities to work with likeminded individuals and companies who share the same mission and values. You can find out more at
www.wiggywam.co.uk

Printed in Great Britain
by Amazon

21030069R00075